The End of Decline

Blair and Brown in Power

The End of Decline

Blair and Brown in Power

Brian Brivati

POLITICO'S

First published in Great Britain 2007 by
Politico's Publishing, an imprint of
Methuen & Co. Ltd
11–12 Buckingham Gate
London
SW1E 6LB

10 9 8 7 6 5 4 3 2 1

A CIP catalogue record for this book is available from the British Library.

ISBN 978-1-84275-171-8

Typeset in Sabon by SX Composing DTP, Rayleigh, Essex
Printed and bound in Great Britain by Biddles Ltd, King's Lynn, Norfolk

For Joe Bailey – friend, inspiration, boss – good luck and happy hunting.

For three friends who pulled me through a long dark tunnel – Gerard, Jane and Philip, and for Meg, who was the light I found at the tunnel's end.

Contents

I can't bear Britain in decline. I just can't.
Margaret Thatcher, interviewed by Michael
Cockerell for BBC TV's Campaign '79,
27 April 1979

Prologue

It was almost as if we looked backward with nostalgia because we could not look forward with hope. And so as the gap between imperial myth and reality grew, so too the view grew that Britain was not, in fact, underpinned by any strong sense of Britishness at all. And it led to a questioning of the very existence of Britain, right across mainstream opinion. Indeed Andrew Marr, now the political editor of the BBC, chose to entitle his 'state of the nation' book *The Day that Britain Died*, writing, 'I have a profound belief in the likelihood of a British union dissolving within a decade.' For Neal Ascherson from the liberal left, all that remains of Britishness is 'a state, a flag and armed forces recruited from every part ... just institutions ... not social reality'. And with a similar eloquence his fellow Scottish writer Tom Nairn has argued that because there was little that is British left to underpin Britain, what he called 'The Break-up of Britain' was inevitable. Professor Linda Colley, whose groundbreaking historical research had demonstrated that the 'United Kingdom' was founded on great but ultimately transient historical forces – the strength of anti-French feeling, the bonds of empire and Protestantism – concludes:

> [...] Recurrent wars with the states of continental Europe have in all likelihood come to an end, so different kinds of Briton no longer feel the same compulsion to remain united in the face of the enemy from without. And crucially, both commercial supremacy and imperial hegemony have gone.

And no more can Britons reassure themselves of their distinct and privileged identity by contrasting themselves with the impoverished Europeans or by exercising authority over manifestly alien people. God has ceased to be British and providence no longer smiles.

And the historian Norman Davies even lists eighteen British institutions which according to him have defined Britishness and which he now suggests have lost their authority, putting the existence of Britain in doubt. And this view of decline and decay – and then a profound sense we have lost our way as a country – is, if anything, held more forcibly today by writers and thinkers from the right – Roger Scruton (whose highly challenging study of Englishness is entitled *An Elegy*), Simon Heffer, Ferdinand Mount. For them the final nails in the coffin of Great Britain are not just devolution but Britain succumbing to multiculturalism and to Europe. For Mount, quoting Orwell that 'England is perhaps the only great country whose intellectuals are ashamed of their own nationality', our nation could become 'one giant cultural mall in which we would all wander, free to choose from a variety of equally valuable lifestyles, to take back and exchange purchases when not given satisfaction or simply to window-shop'. And Melanie Phillips concludes, 'The big political divide in the country is now clear … it is over nothing less than the protection of liberal democracy and the defence of the nation itself.'

Gordon Brown, 7 July 2004[1]

1

Chasing greatness

> The essay reflects what is loved and hated ... It starts not with Adam and Eve but with what it wants to talk about; it says what occurs to it in that context and stops when it feels finished rather than when there is nothing to say.
>
> Theodor Adorno, *Notes to Literature*, vol. 1[1]

If Britain at the beginning of the twenty-first century met Britain at the beginning of the twentieth, in the style of the short story by Jorge Luis Borges called 'The Other',[2] then the conversation they would have might centre on the splendid contradictions of the perennial obsession of British politicians, intellectuals and artists – the great decline debate. In 1905 the British Empire spanned the globe and infant mortality in England and Wales was 138 per 1,000. In 2005 it was 5.1 per 1,000 and Britain was a leading member of the European Union. The younger Britain was riddled with disease, badly housed and badly educated. The older Britain we live in today is comparatively healthy, well (if not actually rather over-) fed, mostly well housed and reasonably educated; yet the young Britain of 1905 felt old and in parts enfeebled and she watched, obsessed, as other states seemed to be doing better than she was.

The conversation between these two characters would begin to get heated when the terms of the debate became subjective:

- What should Britain's role be in the world?
- What should other countries think of Britain?
- What should Britain count for?
- What is Britain?
- Who are the British?

Here the young Britain and the old would clash bitterly as the youthful contradictions of the diseased mind of empire would rant about power, race and mission. The old nation would smile wisely and point out that virtually all the terms of reference that the young country used were out of date almost as soon as they were uttered. The notion of relative decline is not understandable in terms of measuring the wealth of the people: if it were then the debate would have fallen away decades ago. We are all much richer now, as a recent IPPR book put it: 'real GDP per head has increased by more than 283 per cent since 1955 and on average, Britons are almost twice as rich today as they were in 1975'.[3] 'The future', she'd say, 'will be about interdependence and not dominance; future threats are not from other states but from international networks of terrorists carrying chemical weapons and dreadnoughts or nuclear missiles are no use in such a fight.' Young and old would end up quarrelling bitterly and in that quarrel would be manifested much of the intellectual life of this country since 1945.

As we move towards the end of the first decade of the twenty-first century Britain is not 'a young country' but it feels like a new country. Much of the argument that follows is about the conversation described above, but let me begin by talking about the music to which our history has danced. Some countries always dance to marches and their self-confidence is reflected in the driving beat of those tunes. Self-doubt or introspection plays little part in the rhythms they follow. Germany before 1945 was such a state. Britain has always been different. For much of our modern history we listened to the same tunes as Germany and other European nation states and we danced to the music of empire and greatness. But even at the heart of our 'greatness' we had a crisis. Around 1870, the mid-Victorians felt themselves to be slipping both in terms of world position and more existentially in terms of their religion – shaken to the core by the discoveries of Darwin. After victory in the First World War, and especially after victory in the Second, we danced to the music of our own decline – so much so that we became comfortable in those dances, to an extent we started to enjoy them. The argument of this book is quite simply that we don't enjoy that kind of dancing any more. We no longer dance to the music of decline and many of us would no longer even recognise it. We are not a great power according to the traditional and now largely useless old measures. We have become confident, resilient and influential in the exercise of both hard and soft power abroad. In many areas we have become more comfortable, imaginative and successful in how we live together at home – though our model of multiculturalism is in crisis. In almost all ways we live richer and better lives, we consume better-quality products, we enjoy better standards of entertainment. You can walk out of a railway station in virtually any town in the United Kingdom and buy a decent cup of coffee. You can live in Cornwall and work in London using broadband to connect you. Poverty, insecure part-time working and relative deprivation, especially in housing, are still scars on our country but they no longer define it. We are a country that is now envied rather than pitied by other states around the world and we have achieved this through consensus rather than confrontation. In the new measures of greatness that suit a new century we are a great power once more.

What used to be called the British disease had as its symptoms industrial unrest, stop-go policy changes, political polarisation, social unrest, long-term unemployment, high interest rates and higher inflation, poor quality of design and manufacture, dull cultural life, poor external image, unmanageable security threats in parts of the country, separatist aspirations in others, insecurity, ungovernability, white racist superiority and so on. All these have been largely cured, reversed, transformed, managed or incorporated into the governing consensus. We will no doubt mess things up quickly, but we will do so in new kinds of ways.

We cannot understand the role of the Blair–Brown governments* in contributing to this transformation without understanding the legacy of Thatcherism and its impact on British politics and society. But it is Blair and Brown, rather than Margaret Thatcher, who, building on the uneven basis of her legacy, have made Britain the most important power in Europe and one of the most influential players on the world stage and they have aided but did not create a renaissance in British art, culture and design. They have also reversed much (but not enough) of the assertion of white nationalism, xenophobia and Christian-influenced social conservatism that featured increasingly in British political life from the 1980s and they have tapped into a rich vein of widely supported illiberalism on human rights. In sum they have silenced the prophets of doom about the fate of this country in its post-imperial life. From a left-wing perspective much of this has been achieved through a synthesis of policy options that has been forged into a consensus with many progressive elements. These elements coexist with a reactionary strain and illiberal instincts in other areas of policy which, though they might be rejected by progressives,

---

* I refer to the 'Blair–Brown' governments because there was, in essence, a dual premiership between 1997 and 2007.

accurately reflect popular opinion. In doing these things and in the period of government between 1997 and 2003, Tony Blair and Gordon Brown ended the decline debate.

It had been a debate that had mesmerised generations of contemporary historians until it became a demented obsession. The result of this obsession is that there has been little tradition of thinking or writing positively about Britain's recent past, based on the evidence of positive features of that past. I hope that after reading this book, whether they agree with this thesis or not, more people will try to think more positively about our current and recent performance under both Conservative and Labour governments. We need to re-evaluate the more distant past to appreciate the foundations on which our contemporary success rests. In part, we need to do this because the evidence for such a systematic and wide-ranging re-evaluation of Britain's experience since 1945 is overwhelmingly provided by the quality of life we now enjoy. But in part, and more importantly, we need to do this because although the debate is over and the decline has been reversed, politicians have a vested interest in pretending that this is not the case. They have a vested interest in pretending that the kinds of issues that dominated political debate from the 1960s through to the 1990s are still relevant and significant today. That interest lies in the fact that an increasing proportion of the shrinking number of people who bother to vote in elections are over the age of sixty, and the ageing electorate naturally cares about these issues.

Politicians cannot, in the main, tell people what to think. Their power is to tell people what to think about. The tragedy of living in a Britain after decline is that we cannot enjoy it, cannot face the real problems that confront us or prepare properly for the huge challenges of the next hundred years because our political class is terrified of upsetting a small minority whose power is massively magnified because they take the responsibilities of citizenship seriously and go out to vote. Their concerns are not, of course, unimportant. However, they are fighting the last five elections and not the next five elections. The structures of our political institutions and the nature of our political debates allow them to do so.

*

This is a short book on contemporary British history. It is not a full-blown history of the contemporary period or even the Blair–Brown governments. There have been many good post-war histories. Peter Hennessy is slowly working his way towards producing the definitive multi-volume account of our age as viewed from the top down,[4] while David Kynaston's books will provide the view from the ground up.[5] Nor is this is a book about numbers. To judge the record of the Labour government on statistics you should turn to Polly Toynbee and David Walker's excellent books.[6] This is a book about the state of mind of a nation as reflected in the political debates it has about its history. This is not the fashionable liberal and middle-class dinner party attack on New Labour. For that turn to the entertaining polemics of Simon Jenkins[7] or any edition of the *Daily Mail*. It is instead an attempt to evaluate constructively the meaning of the Blair–Brown governments in relation to a broader reading of contemporary British political history and the nature of contemporary politics.

My argument is that in the period between 1997 and 2003 the Labour governments of Tony Blair and Gordon Brown ended the ideological struggle between left and right that had fuelled the long-running debate about Britain's decline. In ending this debate by forming a new consensus, Blair and Brown also produced a rapid and far-reaching modernisation of the mentalities of the British people and of the political culture of the UK. As this new moment became clear, however, it also began to dissolve as the Iraq war and a series of associated scandals broke the political spell that the two leaders had held over the country during the first five years of their government. The country became increasingly racially and politically polarised around issues of identity and security. It did not relapse, however, into any of the various decline discourses that had dominated the great decline debate from the late 1950s onwards.

There are a number of different strands to the decline debate but they all seem to come back, again and again, to the issue of culture. The first is broadly concerned with an analysis of the nature of British political economy. In particular, some of those who wrote about the decline of Britain from the perspective of culture were also concerned with British competitiveness, productivity and the rate of growth in GDP.[8] Such critiques of British performance became widespread after the collapse of Keynesian demand management in the 1970s but they had been present since the late 1950s. The earlier studies also exhibited an intense concern with the fate of the pound as a reserve currency. The second set of works explored economic performance but with a more cultural or identity-based perspective. In the works of writers such as Martin Weiner the position of the currency and the broader debate about British competitiveness became intertwined with what constituted the British, or English, national character. Here a portrait emerged of British values being 'always anti-industrial and normally anti-urban'.[9] These values were nurtured in a public school system that was based, according to Correlli Barnett, another of the leading members of the culturalist camp of declinologists, on a 'remote academicism'[10] which put more emphasis on learning Latin and Greek than on chemistry and physics. These schools championed team sports in which victory was not as important as playing the game, thus producing generations of leaders who were imbued with a sense of conformity and inability to take risks. According to Barnett, the closeness of this life in boarding schools and the romanticism of the classics also bred homosexuality, which 'lastingly and insidiously' influenced the middle and upper classes. Therefore, for Weiner and Barnett, British elite culture was pastoral.

Elites matter, according to Barnett, because they have a

> disproportionate influence upon both the effective climate of opinion and the conduct of affairs. The values of the directing strata, particularly in a stable, cohesive society like Britain, tend to permeate society as a whole and to take on the colour of national values, and of general mentalities . . . bosses tend to get the workers they deserve, the attitudes and behaviours of workers are deeply influenced, even only in reaction, by the attitudes and behaviours of employers.

For the culturalists, these gay, pastoral, anti-industrial elites have played a crucial role in the decline of Britain. Indeed for a long time, the British have not felt comfortable with the idea of 'progress': Barnett goes on: 'The English nation even became ill at ease enough with its prodigal progeny to deny its legitimacy by adopting a conception of Englishness that virtually excluded industrialism.' For Barnett, the values imparted to the future ruling class by their education were probity, orthodoxy, romantic idealism and a strong sense of public responsibility that 'admirably fitted them for running the British Empire as they saw it'.[11]

Much of the culturalist critique appeared in the 1970s and influenced the New Right in their attempt to shift government policy away from the corporatist/interventionist basis of the Labour-inspired political economy of the 1960s. Once

Thatcher was in power there was a reaction against this New Right interpretation of British decline and by the 1980s the debate about decline had shifted to the social costs of deregulation and privatisation. This was conducted in the context of a longer historical view of the decline of the public sector and the civil service.

Neither the culturalist literature nor the responses to it influence discussion today or hold much appeal for critics of the current government. These arguments have no relevance for understanding the contemporary scene and they barely feature in critiques of contemporary political economy.[12] Instead, discussion of how to improve the status of the public sector and public service delivery has been returned to the centre of the political stage. One dimension of the argument of this book is that it was only when public service was returned to the centre and made an object of pride and not derision that the decline of Britain could be talked of in the past tense. Thatcherism's negative attitude to the public services and attempts to reduce public expenditure on them ensured that the sense of decay and decline in schools and hospitals continued to be felt through the 1980s and 1990s. This in turn meant that the everyday conversation about the 'state of the nation' was never really lifted from a continuing sense of crisis, because most people's direct experiences of the state are through schools and hospitals. The 1980s might have appeared to be booming to television executives and city bankers, but for most people the British state remained profoundly sick and the government of the day told them that this state was part of the problem rather than being part of the solution. In the period of the long European peace since 1945, in other words, the way in which a state managed and supported its public services and public institutions provided a more meaningful test of greatness for a nation than the number of tank divisions it had. By 1997 Britain was badly failing the public service test.

The connection between cultural explanations of decline and the reality of relative economic performance lies in the conduct of politics and the nature of education. The 'culturalist' writers, such as Weiner and Barnett, argued that decisions in political economy are shaped by cultural factors. In these works, the nature of a state's education system, the nature of problem solving in the state institutions and the public sector, and the responsiveness of government and the public sector to external changes in the world economy and in the behaviour of other states are all governed by a notion of a national culture informing a national character. According to the culturalists, there might also be cultural dynamics at work in the competitiveness of a state with relation to its openness to language education, which in turn might be an accident of geography as much as a product of culture. They compare the size and the number of drawing boards to suggest that the application of technical, business and management training plays a role in British decline because it feeds the cult of the amateur, this 'cult' being a significant cultural disadvantage for the British when faced, so the argument ran, with the professional and brutal capitalism of the Americans and the corresponding cult of the expert and scientist in Germany.[13] Finally, and related to what some writers have called the British disease, is the nature of inter-class relations as expressed in the work place.[14] These relations, it is claimed, contribute to our understanding of the relation between something we call culture and something we call economic performance. For the culturalists and even for some of their critics such as Ken Coates,[15] the decisions made in Whitehall and Westminster are framed by the culture that is produced by the complex interplay of the factors outlined above.

Writers such as Peter Hennessy[16] come close to suggesting that the role of conformity in Whitehall policy making was a product of British culture and that in fact the role of consensus in political ideology in the UK is merely a reflection of British culture in general. In reality Britain does not have a single national culture or character but many different cultures and characters competing with each other. These diverse identities are shaped by geography, history, religion, gender, sexuality and social class – among other things. Each of these identities has within it elites and masses and the overall elite group in the UK, measured in terms of socio-economic status, job and access to power, is diverse and has its own culture shaped by the conflict between differing norms and values among the many identities this cosmopolitan country is comprised of. From this very complex picture of identity and influence, the culturalists simplify and reduce. For them the evolution of cultural values in society across the century and the impact these have had on our own aspirations and values shape the nature of our political culture. If we can understand that impact we can understand why Britain has declined. In the end this cultural critique really comes down to a critique of mass values: the heart of the Weiner–Barnett thesis as history, and as it was made into politics by Margaret Thatcher, was that we lost our ability to compete because the working class became dependent on welfare. They became dependent on welfare because of the way our class system operated. Our elite was shaped by a public school ethos that was agrarian, classically orientated and anti-scientific and therefore became seduced away from enterprise towards socialism. This 'decline of the industrial spirit' literature and its associated works that talk of a people hanging on the nipple of state paternalism seem absurdly old fashioned today. The very notion of a national character or a single British culture seems an oddly antediluvian way of understanding political action or economic success. This book will argue that it was the Blair–Brown governments and the synthesis they produced that made these ideas seem so far fetched.

The absurdity of the national character or culture thesis is most starkly illustrated with respect to our world role. In each of these decades and stretching back to the 1940s there has been a recurrent discussion about Britain's position in the world. Winston Churchill argued that Britain should sit at the centre of three interconnected circles – Europe, United States and the Empire or Commonwealth. The trick in the post-war period would be not to plunge into any one of these circles to the exclusion of the others. On a strategic plane this problem has remained the same ever since. Economically, Europe has become much more central to Britain's future than the other two but the political arguments about what the nature of our relationship with Europe should be have remained fraught with difficulties. This agonising over the politics of Europe stands in marked contrast to our increasingly confident, complex and unapologetic cultural connection with the continent: from holidays through fashion and football to food and literature we are a European civilisation.

This in turn raises the broader comparative element of the debate on Britain's supposed economic decline and how that might be accounted for and the role of the public services and the public sector in causing that decline.[17] Put simply, Britain has been doing better economically and to an extent socially than France and Germany for about a decade. Strategically, however, the question of whether Britain should be an Atlantic power or a European one, and whether it should use soft power or hard power in the global war on terrorism, remains acute. But note that this is a debate about the nature of the role Britain will play in the world, the depth of our partnership with the USA in the global war on terrorism, the dimensions of a European alternative and Britain's part in that, the extent of our commitment on development and Third World debt and so on. It is not a debate, outside fringe isolationists of the extreme left and the extreme right, about whether we should play this role in the world at all.

Relative decline is, by definition, absolute growth – but can a people or a culture be more or less great? Is that an absolute condition? British culture was for decades permeated with ideas of failure. Our libraries are packed with volumes examining our decline from imperial greatness and until recently our politics were dominated by people obsessed with reversing a century of change or, in the case of Margaret Thatcher, claiming that they had. 'Decline' should be understood as a self-perpetuating cultural phenomenon and political weapon rather than a continuing political problem. It is a vainglorious obsession with ill-defined and frequently contradictory notions of the might-have-beens of history. The final adjustment to our post-1945 status in the world must be to historicise the decline debate. Indeed, the decline school of contemporary British history has been silenced by the New Labour government. This in turn should make us rethink the history of Britain since 1945.

This is not to suggest that all our problems have been solved. While many of the old set of problems have been dealt with, there are new ones and they are just as difficult and challenging, especially in terms of the identity of the British people and quite what our strategic role in the world should be. But we do not face them with the same sense of pessimism and failure that we have tended to exhibit since the late 1950s. So how has Labour pulled off the trick of ending the decline debate without solving any of the profoundest questions of identity and our global position? It has done this by returning politics to the pattern of consensus removed from the extremes that characterised the 1950s and other periods of British success. Dynamic change and political dialectics gave way to the comfortable peace of a broadly contented nation. It fell apart again, as all periods of success do. The political stability and consensus of the 1950s, after all, was unchallenged only until the Suez crisis of 1956. But it fell apart in new ways and not old. The great decline debate, the 'sick man of Europe', the 'British disease' were all made history by Tony Blair and Gordon Brown; the new debates of a new era have begun.

When G. M. Trevelyan wrote that the British soldier in the trenches of the First World War could have understood the conversation and appreciated the values of the British soldier fighting Napoleon, he might have been right – though I doubt it. The argument between old and young Britain on the park bench would, no doubt, have ended in a shouting match rather than mutual admiration. The level of incomprehension between young and old, between 1905 Britain and 2005 Britain, would have been such that shouting would be the only possible outcome to the conversation. They could have understood each other's words, recognised some of the core values and been familiar in outline with the institutions of the British state and the roles they play, but they could not have understood the changes in life experiences, expectations and styles.

2

The great decline debate

Before filling out my argument for a reappraisal of the post-war period and the impact of the Blair–Brown governments, I want to discuss what the great decline debate actually was and how it might fit into a longer-run understanding of the course of British history. As I have already suggested, for much of the period since 1945 British historians have written as though the end of their world was nigh. British historiography described and reflected on a picture of seemingly endless decline, crisis and decay and fought within itself as to whether broadly based class and institutional reasons might be to blame or if it were merely the people involved. A few years ago in the *Contemporary History Handbook*,[1] I wrote about the evolution of schools of contemporary British history. That discussion offers a background to understanding the great decline debate.

The decline school of historical writing grew out of a rejection of the old Whig interpretation of history, in which the story of Britain was the endless march of progress. There were two kinds of response to the collapse of the Whiggish view of the past. On the left the history of classes and structures replaced the history of men and measures. As Richard Brent has put it:

> [social history's] deleterious effect was to confine 'politics', as traditionally understood, to the status of peripheral activity or epiphenomenon. This second school of writing was equally linear in outlook, but instead of telling the story of the rise of

political institutions [as the Whig interpretation had done], it told of the rise of classes or groups, of which political developments were simply a reflexion.[2]

The second school, coming broadly from the right, is known as the high-politics or Cambridge school. The historian Ross McKibbin once condemned one of the products of the Cambridge school as 'a rather large book' based 'almost exclusively on gossip'.[3]

The ideas of the Cambridge school, as viewed by critics such as McKibbin, were a rejection of the notion that politics was either about the triumph of liberalism or determined by socio-economic factors. The school stressed ambition as the motive of political action and manoeuvre as the occupation of politicians, and believed that the activity of parliamentary politics was discrete, impervious to changes in the world outside Westminster, and that politicians competed solely for office. Therefore any movement away from the House of Commons as the central focus of political life was the beginning of the end of the British way of life.

In analysing the Cambridge school Brent stated that 'public opinion mattered, but it appeared on the political stage not as a directing agent, manipulating the actors, but as a piece of scenery or prop, at times useful to politicians, at others hindering their ability to move across the stage'. Moreover, Westminster was a closed world 'like Whitehall or the City' and not the top of a pyramid of power resting in the people. In such a world politics was conducted as a private game 'in which the object was office and success, rather than some conception of the welfare of the nation'. Brent clearly states the partisan nature of the high-politics school but maintains that it does not really matter that this school 'was as much in danger of constructing false idols and dogmatic history as its liberal rivals'.[4] What mattered was 'their rejection of certain languages of explanation, rather than the substitution of one set of partisan historical conclusions by another. In particular this school was distinguished by its opposition to the possibility of a scientific (and it believed liberal) study of politics.' Politics was a craft and not a science; therefore it could not be taught but only learnt: 'The only school of political practice is the conversation of those who govern.' In conversation with the past the historian would discover some of the story of politics. It was therefore essential to search out as much of this conversation as possible:

> It was thought that only in the intimacy of politicians' diaries, personal correspondences and notes did the scholar have the faintest chance of engaging in a truthful colloquy on the art of the politician . . . [because] power is exercised and decisions are made not by vast movements of opinion but specifically by individual men.

Politics in this way was not very different from any other walk of life.

This evolution of British historical writing into the high-politics school reached its peak in the late 1970s and early 1980s. The focus in these works was very much the 'conversation of those who govern'. The response to the high-politics school developed in the social history school by writing about the relative deprivation of the British people, the poverty of the welfare state and the weakness of the developmental state. The two wings came together in arguing for the importance of culture in understanding the nature of the decline of Britain. The interplay between the academic historians was reflected in popular books and frequent editorials so that for more than forty years, from 1955 to 1997, the decline debates mesmerised the British elite; indeed, these were the national conversations. In understanding why, we can also understand why the debate has now finally been ended by the New Labour governments.

The complexity of our obsession with relative decline was in part derived from the nature of our thinking and writing classes: thus the first layer of what we might call the culture of decline was influenced by the concerns of those who shape and interpret our culture. This elite group, from the art broadcaster Kenneth Clark in the 1950s through to Jeremy Paxman's and John Humphrys's musings on Englishness and language today, are obsessed by the issue. The fragmentation of intellectual life in this country reflects and is a reflection of a subtle set of competing hierarchies, each with a contrasting view of the central debate of contemporary British history. Traditionally, these different hierarchies have been described as left and right, democratic socialist and conservative. When thinking about decline, however, there are at least three other kinds of divide that can make as much sense – town versus country, north versus south, England versus the other nations. There can also be even more specialised divides such as those who champion Cabinet over Prime Minister, or Parliament over both. But for all of these groups, at the heart of the debate is an idea of British power – who has it and how should it be used.

The nineteenth-century liberal notion of British power as a force for good illustrates the layers of contradiction inherent in almost all features of these debates. First, British power was a force for good in terms of the spreading of Christianity. Later, the more liberal notion developed of Britain being the conveyor of democracy. Throughout, ideas about British power were underpinned by the search for profit and the 'power imperialism' idea of empire. Imperialism was disguised in a cassock of moral force but this did not obscure the fact that Britain needed to be a Great

Power fundamentally for reasons of realpolitik (long before Bismarck made such a concept commonplace). In turn, these notions about the nature of British power were in essence cultural because they were tied directly to the idea of the special nature of the British people and nation. If there is a decline in the power of the nation state there must by definition be a decline in the strength and character of the people and the nation, or so this argument goes. As we will see later the evolution of these notions of power and of the nature of the British people played out during the twentieth century in the context of a dynamic British political system capable of rapid change and effective adaptability.

Wrapped up in this notion of British power that we will return to a number of times in this book are a number of different dimensions to the idea of decline. As I have just argued, there is the idea of the decline of Britain being concerned with the decline of these islands as a moral force in the world, as an educator of the un-Christian globe. In turn there is the idea of Westminster as the mother of parliaments and Britain as the civilising force of political liberalism and the spreader of democratic values – a neocon agenda a century early. Finally, there is the idea of Britain deteriorating in her capability to find new sources of profit and leading to her decline as the dominant economic power. In each case the notion of a relative decline is difficult to untangle. Christianity was superseded within the British political tradition rather than being defeated by some alternative religious or moral force. The notion of democracy advocated by Victorian liberals had little in common with the notion of democracy planned by the Colonial Development Corporation or the Fabian Bureau. The contradictions between the liberal idea of empire as a force for improvement challenged the twentieth-century notion of self-determination, leading to the confused notions of the interwar

Colonial Office and the inherent moral contradiction of colonial development. These outward-looking questions were separate again from the metropolitan debate, a debate which was centred on the idea that empire made Britain great at home and in comparison with other European powers. For this to be true empire was necessary so long as it served to perpetuate greatness. Each idea of British power was mingled with a separate racist and patriotic strand that argued that Britain was great and should be great because the British were intrinsically great as a people. For decline to be meaningful here the British race must in some sense have declined while other races triumphed. Given the complexity and richness of contradictions in the notion of greatness it is not difficult to see why decline has dominated the intellectual and political life of this country for much of the period since the Second World War.

Central to the notion of relative decline is an 'other' who has in some sense done better than we have. There are two key ghosts at the feast of British decline: Germany and the United States. At each level of our culture and politics sits the idea and memory of Germany. For some the great failure of Britain in the twentieth century is that we were not German, and the high priest of this view is Correlli Barnett. The central contradiction in this world view is that while Germany is held up as some sort of ideal – an ideal which changes through time – it is also despised for its very success and feared as a potential threat. For every Alan Clark in love with the German army, there is an Andrew Roberts writing novels about a German-led super-state. But it was not only those on the 'right' who looked wistfully at Germany. In their excellent studies of decline and the declinists, Richard English and Michael Kenny illustrate the obsession with Germany with the following story:

A pertinent example is the late Sidney Pollard's sense that while Britain squandered multiple opportunities in the post-war period, the German penchant for state investment ensured rapid and effective modernisations: 'Very soon after I came to Sheffield in the early 1950s there was a great campaign to link the university with local industry. The industrialists came to the university and we were led round the works, and I could see what steel works looked like. And then sometime later I went round German works and found myself in a different world. And it was obvious that our people could not produce and expand at the rate the Germans could.'[5]

The post-war period has seen the painful process of watching Germany rise from her ideal position, prostrate at our feet as an occupied power, through division and economic reconstruction, to reunification and economic recovery. Unpacking these fears – rational and irrational – requires an exploration of the heart of the right's nationalism. There is a deep confusion, a crisis of identity and a complex love–hate relationship with Germany. At the heart of this is an abstract notion of her which is constructed from a mixture of history, film and invented collective memories. It is a relationship which is almost as complex as that with the USA. In relation to the USA, the problem is even deeper. The British race has failed the nation because its spirit has been perverted by the guiles of American capitalism and the seductions of American culture.

If differences of language and culture affect our relations and perceptions of Germany, similarities have formed our notion of the USA. At some point in the 1950s we stopped measuring ourselves against only US standards and began to measure ourselves against Europe as well. British culture, with short exceptions in the 1960s and 1990s, had an inbuilt inferiority complex towards European culture which caused it to turn inwards. This moment in the 1950s was complex. What remained true, despite the increasing intrusion of Europe into our consciousness, was a stubborn belief that our relationship with the USA was qualitatively different from anyone else's.

The declinologists who specialise in the Special Relationship – that curious phrase which presupposes that there is something unique about our ties to the USA – face the harshest challenge. The presentation of the Special Relationship as a meaningful experience in the post-war world relies on the meaning invested in the term 'influence'. If we were Greeks to the Americans' Romans then we have to ask ourselves: which policies did the USA follow or not follow because of our influence? Though a shared language and intertwined history matter, there was little else to separate the Anglo-American relationship with the ties between the USA and a dozen other countries until 9/11. On a range of issues – withdrawal east of Suez, nuclear technology, policy in the Middle East and shared intelligence on the Soviet Union – we kidded ourselves that our relations with the USA were in some sense unique, when in fact they were based on realpolitik judgements from both sides of the Pond. Wilson staying out of Vietnam and Reagan keeping benevolently neutral during the Falklands War illustrate the point. Unpacking the idea of these special links, before 9/11, reveals a deeply unflattering picture of the posturing of the mid-Atlantic intellectuals whose pretensions have been repeatedly exposed by the realities of power in the post-war world. After 9/11 things are different and a Special Relationship clearly does exist – for good or ill.[6]

While some thinkers defined the problem comparatively by identifying an 'other', another group of thinkers have defined the problem internally: they call it the British disease and they feel it. They do not argue that British culture has let the nation down, but rather lament that something called the British nation has not been strong enough to withstand the onslaught of modernity. Nostalgia is not enough to define this group; it is more that, feeling an intense form of patriotism but lacking a crude right-wing language with which to express it, they internalise their feelings about the way Britain has slipped and such feelings surface in their writing and broadcasting. This group, with Peter Hennessy being the leading liberal and Simon Heffer the leading conservative, are responsible for the narrative of decline: they tell the story. They do this partly as therapy, partly out of necessity, but also with an underlying sense that nothing will, can or should change. For them, underneath British failure there is genius, the British genius – or perhaps that failure is the British genius. This manifests itself in many ways, some of which deserve our genuine respect, but it is perhaps clearest in the glorification of the unwritten constitution, summed up in the title of one of Hennessy's books, *Muddling Through* – a celebration of the fact that the irrational basis of power in the British political system allows the back-of-an-envelope mentality of the amateur into the very heart of government.

A more specialised group whose time has come and gone were the prophets of colonial development. For them the British Empire – and by extension British 'greatness' – could be saved by reaching out to it, and later the Commonwealth, and bringing it along, educating it – helping it to grow up. The civil servants who inhabited the Colonial Office in the interwar period and dreamed up schemes for developing and maturing the colonies so that they could take on the task of being 'mature' democracies had an answer to decline and an alternative model of the future. There is a novel by Michael Moorcock in which the airship does not go into decline but becomes the means of imperial control for an enlightened form of British Empire. In this vision and in the vision of the colonial developers, the colonies become a series of little Englands. These were a class of people trained to run an empire which evaporated in front of them.

As the empire receded the state grew. The crisis, the disease, was not caused by the cultural poverty of Britain, another school of declinists argued, or the loss of empire, but by choices based on the way we organised our political economy. This school of writing began with Michael Shanks's seminal *The Stagnant Society*[7] and was developed in Anthony Sampson's *Anatomy of Britain* series.[8] It reached its height in the body of literature that argued that Britain had become ungovernable in the 1970s and was replaced with more positivist blueprints for the reform of institutions and the introduction of a written constitution in the 1980s and 1990s. David Marquand, Will Hutton and other gurus of decline reversal worked out complex plans for modernising and turning back the tides of economic depression and societal failure. Putting the state in has dominated their thinking because, though not always practitioners, they believe in politics. They believe in politics because they are the last Victorians. They believe in the ability of the state, a small well-run state perhaps, to make the right laws to create the circumstances in which Britain can be great. For these statists culture is malleable. In their view it is possible to, in some sense, save the nation by creating the development state that will in turn shape a culture that can compete in the global market place.

The blueprints of the intellectuals of decline have been taken up with gusto by generations of politicians whose business was and is to make the concrete decisions that would reverse that decline. There has developed a distinct group of British politicians since the war who are concerned with ideas and with the larger questions but who have also pursued successful ministerial careers. These politicians generally become fixated on a particular ideological response to change through time. As English and Kenny have shown, for example,

the Thatcherite attempt to change a perceivedly pervasive anti-business prejudice in Britain, and to resurrect a once vibrant 'enterprise culture', borrowed from and resonated with the arguments of some intellectuals prominent in decline debates. Martin Wiener's *English Culture and the Decline of the Industrial Spirit* (1981) provides an example, with Keith Joseph (himself an influential political intellectual) famously deploying Wienerite arguments . . . Similarly, Correlli Barnett's declinist theses were employed by Conservative politicians who sought a long-term change from what they saw as policies and attitudes that had caused British decline . . . Thatcherites sought to uproot practices and to challenge institutions which had, in their view, exacerbated 'the British disease'. If, as has recently been suggested, such people 'saw both the country and the Conservative Party as having taken a wrong turning in and after 1945 as a consequence of misreading the 1930s' . . . then it is clear why Barnett's hostility to the 1940s welfare project might appeal. Moreover, Wiener and Barnett's criticisms of established elites clearly resonated with Thatcherite hostility towards elite sections of British society. Declinist motifs are not the sole preserve of Thatcherites, however. This theme has been deployed across the spectrum of Conservative thought and politics, in part because it permits the articulation of anxieties about the fate of the United Kingdom state as well as the changing configuration of national identities within it.[9]

The free-market right can be represented by Keith Joseph and John Biffen, the nationalist right by Enoch Powell, who came to be the leader of a significant section of British opinion that was anti-immigrant, and one-nation Toryism by Edward Boyle, a Cabinet minister who seemed to personify that tradition. To illustrate the kinds of position taken let us consider Joseph, once dismissed by Ian Gilmour as 'a Rolls-Royce brain without a chauffeur' and by Harold Macmillan as 'the only boring Jew I've ever met'.[10] Joseph's intellectual journey through government and opposition led him famously to declare that he became a Conservative in 1974 when he understood the nature of the state and of inflation.[11] For Joseph British decline had been caused by the state and its mistakes in political economy:

> Inflation is threatening to destroy our society. It is threatening to destroy not just the relative prosperity to which most of us have become accustomed, but the savings and plans of each person and family and the working capital of each business and other organisation. The distress and unemployment that will follow unless the trend is stopped will be catastrophic. There is a risk, moreover, that political parties which preside with well-intentioned ineffectiveness over such a universal frustration of expectations will pave the way for those who will offer solutions at the cost of freedoms. It has happened elsewhere. It could happen here. Our proud achievements, our great history, our still superb national talents do not render us immune to the processes of despair and disintegration which ultimately invite dictatorship. Our fate lies in our own hands. If we recognise the nightmares which galloping inflation brings, we can abate it. It is a question of priorities. Mr Heath and Mr Carr and all of us say that inflation is the most important issue before the country. We say this, not only because inflation destroys jobs by destroying employers, not only because it savages the vast majority of our population in their savings and plans, but also

because all other social and economic objectives will be lost unless inflation is abated. Growth, social peace, full employment, regional balance, social services – no one of these aims can be sustained if inflation is allowed to continue at its present or anything like its present pace. But, you may ask, if inflation is so pernicious, why was it allowed to get a grip in the first place?

Though Joseph blamed inflation above everything else for the failure of the British economy in the period since 1945, his critique extended beyond one economic indicator to encompass the overall role of the state, as he continued:

Why did successive governments for the last score years, led by well-intentioned and intelligent people advised by conscientious officials and economists, take a course which led inexorably and predictably to the present nightmare? I say predictably, because there were warnings as far back as 1950, charting with painful accuracy the course on which the country embarked. Political and economic historians will pronounce in due course. As a participant in the process, I may lack their perspective. But at least I know how things seemed to us, why we acted as we did, and with the vision of hindsight where we went astray. So, as a participant, retracing my steps seems the best introduction to the problem. I begin by accepting my full share of the collective responsibility. It is not right for government to claim credit for what goes well unless they accept their share of the blame for what goes badly. For over the past thirty years governments in this country have had unprecedented power over economic life. It is only fair that we should accept correspondingly heightened responsibility for what has gone wrong.[12]

Joseph became a force behind Margaret Thatcher when she became leader of the Conservative Party in 1975, and she was clear that her task in government was to reverse decline. At a press briefing during her first foreign visit as Prime Minister, to France, she was asked by David Lawday of the *Economist*: 'The French normally when they are talking about this relationship come up with phrases like "Britain is lacking in vision". How did you reassure Giscard on the point that Britain might have vision?' She replied:

> That was what I was elected to give. With a little resolve perhaps . . . we cannot in the middle of Paris refight the British election over again. Well, we could have done, but we didn't. But obviously my views, my economic views, are very well known. We have to turn Britain round from being a wealth-distributing country to being a wealth-creating country. For years the emphasis has been on wealth distribution and we really just have not got stuck into the problems of wealth creation. Hence the basic reason for the decline compared with our European neighbours. It does mean a different attitude towards taxation. I won't explain to you any further on that; you will be hearing a good deal more by this time next week . . . I am there to turn around the economy of Britain so I hope we shall have more influence in the world . . . If you are a declining country, you just don't carry the clout that a successful country does.[13]

This is one of the many examples of Thatcher's personal obsession with the idea of decline. This obsession gradually translated in her mind and in the mind of her followers into the idea that she had reversed decline, that she had made Britain great again. Her notion of the decline that Britain had reversed was locked into the image of a failed entrepreneurial people, let down by the state and socialism. It was about the competitiveness of the private sector and its ability to replace the public sector. For this reason alone she cannot be said to have ended the decline debate because of the absence of the public sector and public services from her thesis, which is an idea I will return to later.

Each of these Conservative politicians seemed to feel the idea of the decline of Britain deeply and each offered their own differing explanations for it. They came together in the rhetoric in which they articulated their blueprints for reversing it – broadly the decline of Britain would be reversed by taking the state out of running the economy and ultimately 'society' as well – therefore undermining and downplaying the importance of the public sector (explicitly) and the public services (implicitly).

On the left, Aneurin Bevan, Anthony Crosland, Tony Benn and Peter Shore represented a spectrum of collectivist responses connected by patriotism and a belief in the possibility of reversing decline through various kinds of interventions ranging from nationalisation to rejuvenated Keynesianism – broadly they wanted to put more of the state in. English and Kenny see the left's connection to decline rather differently:

> In some ways, left-inclined intellectuals might be thought less obviously suited to declinist engagement. Can they, for example, lament the decline of imperial power, of monarchical glory, or of capitalist economic dominance? The answer is that a rather different set of declinist narratives has clustered at this end of the political spectrum. One intriguing and influential engagement has been that developed by the New Left intellectuals Perry Anderson and Tom Nairn, and first expounded in an important series of articles in the 1960s ... Their reading of British historical development presumed that this polity was unique for the absence of a truly

bourgeois revolutionary moment. Consequently, the aristocracy had absorbed the emergent industrial bourgeoisie from the early 19th century onwards, and had ruled within a state form that remained *ancien régime* in character. In an account which has been widely echoed in intellectual circles, the advantages that had once rendered Britain the leading economic and military power during the industrial revolution turned into features that constrained progress once new competitors appeared on the international scene in the late 19th century. By the 1960s, the incapacity of the British state to modernise its institutional and constitutional architecture was seen by Anderson and other New Left intellectuals as a clear indication of the pathology that had been established in this earlier era.[14]

In turn, social democratic intellectuals, such as David Marquand, focused directly on the state in the sense of wanting to make it more developmental, and those on the far left focused on the state as the instrument for running a siege economy in the face of the imminent collapse of world capitalism. There are many examples that could be used to illustrate the picture that English and Kenny paint; here is Tony Benn in full flow in 1980:

> The starting point must be what is happening now: how did we get here, and how do socialists respond in a way that is successful? First, how do we defend the interests of those we try to represent? Secondly, how do we enlarge the political consciousness of our own people? How do we campaign for change? Hilary Wainwright, in my opinion, put the most important question of all, which is: how do you interrelate the efforts of people at their place of work to the work of the trade unions and the political parties at national level, and above all, when you've got a support how do you carry it

through? To have had a discussion without any reference to the fact that Britain is caught in a world slump with a weakened capitalist system and with deliberate policy of deindustrialisation would be to leave out the background against which we meet and to miss the major problem that we now have to discuss: the fact that we have a capitalist system in this country which is no longer capable of sustaining the welfare upon which so much of our post-war politics rested. The real problem is not that the Tory government are pursuing their policy, but that there is no alternative to their policy unless we are prepared to achieve a 'fundamental and irreversible shift in the balance of wealth and power in favour of working people and their families', if I may be allowed to quote myself, for I am myself responsible for setting that objective for the Labour movement in 1973.[15]

In other words, the private sector is failing. The answer to this failure is not, for Benn and other leftists, a reform of the way the private sector operates in the context of global competitiveness but rather a massive increase in the public sector to remove it from competing in that 'failed' global market place:

The last Labour government, within the framework of market forces, did try to protect the people it sought to represent. It is no good pretending that there is no difference between the Thatcher policy and the policy of successive Labour governments, because if you do that you destroy the credibility upon which support must rest. The Labour government did, in some respects, shift the balance of power by the repeal of the Industrial Relations Act and by erecting the Health and Safety Act and the Employment Protection Act.

The reality is that we have come as far as can possibly be advanced within the basically capitalist system. Indeed we have come now to the point where the capitalist system cannot even allow us to sustain the gains that were made before. It is true that socialists, both inside and outside the Labour Party, have said all this before. It is the role of socialists to look ahead, and our privilege to be proved right. But I would say this to colleagues who are not members of the Labour Party: to forecast the future correctly is not the same as to forecast the remedies that would succeed in changing that future. That is the great difficulty that we confront. If the Labour Party has not achieved socialism, neither have the socialist groups. It would be a great mistake if we were to pretend at this meeting that this is just a matter of allocating blame and then going home and starting all over again.

I am not here to ask for your support for me. What I am saying is that the Labour Party has made formidable gains since 1945 in the maintenance of full employment, the development of the welfare state, the extension of public ownership and the establishment of trade union rights. I accept that much of this was the unfinished business of the 1906 Liberal government but it laid the foundations for welfare capitalism, which had a profound effect upon a significant section of the Labour Party in diverting them from socialism.

Joseph and Benn shared a penchant for trashing the record of the governments in which they had served, a luxury many civil servants might well have enjoyed. While politicians set out ways of trying to reverse decline, civil servants managed it. There are two main groups of civil servants of decline: the colonialists, whom we have already discussed, and the economists. The latter have had two main concerns: the search for growth and the defence of sterling. In neither of these policy areas did their blueprints, their Whitehall-knows-best attitude, completely fail. The British economy grew and the pound was defended but, equally, in neither area could the ghosts in the machine actually succeed in defending Britain from the realities of the world economy and world markets. The obsession with the status of the pound as a reserve currency and then as an independent one still exists at the time of writing. The economic decision to stay out of the single European currency seems to have been sound but it was only an economic decision. Like earlier debates about the gold standard, convertibility and devaluation, the status and importance attached to the position of a national currency in a globalised world seems quixotic on a hard-nosed realpolitik level. Many would have opposed joining the euro even if the economic argument could have been made, just as in 1964 many opposed devaluation. Currencies are symbols, like tank divisions and kings and presidents, of what makes a state what it is. But in a global economy and a nuclear world, they are as meaningless as the number of Chieftain tanks we have.

In the Wonderland of the decline debate the currency was a touchstone of political seriousness and ideological position. The key to the status of the currency in these debates is the way in which it combines the three core elements of what measures a nation's relative position. A currency seems to connect in many people's perceptions with a country's status as a world power. This is not altogether silly in the case of the pound of course, because for much of the twentieth century the sterling area made up a significant part of the world economy. But the cost of trying to maintain that status long after it was sustainable is connected to the second major site of these debates, political economy. It was an embedded idea in the understanding of how the British economy functioned that the pound as a global currency had to be supported. The process of gradually dismantling this fixed idea, over decades, did a great deal of the groundwork that made the Thatcher revolution possible. But neither global position nor political economy can really explain the centrality of this issue over time and in very different kinds of political contexts. Here we need to think again about culture and more precisely identity.

The third great theme of the decline debate, and one that permeates the others, is the question of identity. Who do we think we are? Who do *they* think we are? The clearest image I have to introduce this question of identity concerns not the currency but a passport. Britain joined the EEC finally in 1973 and eventually signed all the major treaties thereafter – with some caveats. The treaty to create the European Union created a dual characteristic to how people feel about their status. They might accept the legal position that they are citizens of the EU but they also cling to the idea that they are subjects of the Queen. Our passports needed to be redesigned for the purpose of recognising the new legal position and the maroon EU passport was introduced to replace the old hardcover blue UK one. I remember an item on the television show *Points of View*, reacting to the news coverage of the issuing of the new passports, in which a middle-aged man with a Home Counties accent held up the new passport and spat venom at it, a bit like Charlie Chaplin in *The Great Dictator*: 'This is not a British passport.' What struck me then and stays with me now is the force of the passion he directed at this bureaucratic tool. He should really have resented the existence of a passport at all. Instead he had made the blue leather-bound version a badge of his identity. Perhaps this chap is one of those who now buy the fake leather covers in which to hide their citizenship of the EU.

The literature of decline

Questions of political economy, world power status and identity dominated the debate because they were arguments about things that were happening. They were not responsible for all of the literature produced in the endless discussion of the state of the nation. We have already met some of these groups but let me lay out the list more fully. There were those, whom I will call the 'Attleeites and Churchillians', who felt a simple nostalgia for the past and wrote this up as historical or political analysis. Then there were the 'Doppelgängers', who were certain and specific about the model, initially Germany and later south-east Asia, that Britain should copy in every detail to save our greatness. And there were the 'Powellites and Confessionals', for whom it was race and Protestantism that needed protecting. Specific groups also pleaded a special interest as victims of British decline. Trade unionists moaned either about the failure of government to do their bidding or about the way they were being blamed for the British disease and made scapegoats for economic failure. Civil servants agonised over their status and independence, and the decline of the once-great civil service became one barometer of the world that was lost. Others blamed the loss of empire on the emphasis on classical education as a preparation for public service, or took the opposite view that it was the decline in classical education that led to that position. Even the monarchy featured in the blame game; for some, the more we knew about the royal family, the deeper our malaise seemed to be.

But it was not merely political writers, journalists and broadcasters who were engaged in and with this decline debate. We have also lived in a culture of decline. Post-war British literature is littered with characters that are the casualties of Britain's decline. Orwell's nightmare visions of *Nineteen Eighty-Four* and *Animal Farm* are warnings of the inherited British values that need to be saved, as much as *The Lion and the Unicorn* is a celebration of the inherently contradictory features of Britain that Orwell wanted preserved. Decline was personalised in the traitors and

betrayers of Graham Greene, in the intellectual failures of
C. P. Snow and his two cultures, and in the emotional cripples
of Anthony Powell's *A Dance to the Music of Time*. The spy
genre articulated particularly clearly what it felt like to watch
the slippage in British prestige as the Americans moved
inexorably into each former British sphere of influence and
the occupants of the circus sat silent and watched:

> *George Smiley:* In my time, Peter Guillam, I've seen Whitehall
> skirts go up and come down again. I've listened to all the
> excellent argument for doing nothing, and reaped the
> consequent frightful harvest. I've watched people hop up and
> down and call it progress. I've seen good men go to the wall
> and the idiots get promoted with a dazzling regularity. All I'm
> left with is me and thirty-odd years of Cold War without the
> option.
> *Peter Guillam:* So what does that mean, in little words?
> *George Smiley:* It means that if a rogue elephant (to use Saul
> Enderby's happy phrase) charges at me out of the thicket of
> my past and gives me a second shot at it, I intend to shoot it
> dead – but with the minimum of force.[16]

The painful disintegration of the British spy world created
in John Le Carré's stories is soothed by the misogynist cartoon
antics of Ian Fleming's James Bond. The utter ruthlessness of
Bond, a semi-autobiographical rendering of how Fleming
wished he could have behaved himself, is designed to show
that the individual Englishman can save the world even if the
Americans actually run the place. But Bond is also, like the
stars of *The Avengers* and other series of the kind produced in
the 1960s, super-smart and very posh. In other words these
works of fiction are painting a picture of the British elite that
is the mirror opposite of the image portrayed in the culturalist
accounts. These cartoon characters are not pastoral, gay and

soft. They are metropolitan, aggressively heterosexual and hard – though they might have exhibited a certain campness at times. In these genres they remain British and try to reclaim greatness for the British character. Implicit in Smiley's world is the notion that it was socialism that had produced the rot. This idea is taken to its logical conclusion in works that imply that the 'British' spirit has been exported to the colonies. In the Nevil Shute novel *In the Wet*, a socialist Britain is about to get rid of the Queen when she is rescued by some rugged, independent and tough-minded Australian and Canadian pilots. The Queen moves 'the Firm', and by implication the spirit of England, out of the declining socialist dystopia to new utopia of the dominions:

> So that was what was in the wind. There was to be a Governor-General in England as in all the other Dominions, a buffer between the elected politicians and the Queen, selected by the Queen for his ability to get on with the politicians of the day while serving her . . . it meant that she would leave England herself almost immediately; she would hardly remain in the country after the appointment . . . The shock to the British people would be immense . . . The distinctive Australian Air Force uniform might prove a liability; an Australian aeroplane might be exposed to sabotage.[17]

These kinds of story are superseded in the 1980s and 1990s by a brash and ultimately hollow literature of personal aggrandisement at the cost of personal and emotional integrity, in the work of writers such as Martin Amis, Julian Barnes, Irvine Welsh and others. The extent to which decline emasculates the culture of British literature is shown clearly in the extent to which there are no great post-war political novels. Alongside the literature of hedonism and the

celebration of the chemical generation, there developed
genres of non-fiction that contained coded though obvious
attacks on individualism, that are riddled with nostalgia for
a vanished collectivist Britain. Often these are memoirs of
childhoods in areas of deprivation, for example *The Road to
Nab End*.[18]

Though novels, films and television series are works of art
they often, obviously, reflect the wider conversations and
concerns of a country and its culture. In fiction it is possible
to play with the past and the present and visualise different
fates for Britain in the post-war world. But this wishful
thinking drifts across into bodies of literature that exist in an
uneasy no man's land between fiction and non-fiction,
between polemic and critical analysis and between political
manifesto and rant. Writers such as Correlli Barnett argue
that we won the Second World War but lost the peace; that
after 1945 our island story was of the putrefaction of a once-
great nation state, a once-great race; that, as he puts it in the
memorable conclusion to *The Audit of War*, our working
class latched onto the 'nipple of state paternalism'.[19] Our
empire and world role were squandered, they cross over into
this twilight zone. Beyond Barnett the claims made for what
happened to Britain in the post-war years and the theories
presented for reversing this decline get increasingly batty: the
EEC becomes a German plot to refight the Second World
War through subsidies, the decimalisation of the currency
represents the end of civilisation as we know it, the metric
system is designed to destroy Britain's manufacturing base,
and so on. All these have been used to account for the sad
demise of Albion.

The great decline debate, as described above, was a form
of conversation about the past. The conversation was,
moreover, used to influence the shape of the present. There
were different elements in the debate. There was the question

of British power. There were discussions of the nature of a national culture. There was the conceptual issue of the relationship between relative and absolute decline or progress. There was much discussion of the responsiveness of the British state to change. There were diametrically opposed views on the impact of the great modernising projects of Clement Attlee and Margaret Thatcher, which need to be put into a broader historical context to be understood fully. In the overview that follows I want to try and suggest a reading of British history in the twentieth century that picks out some of these elements and debates. We will then consider the two great modernising projects of the contemporary era in relation to individual citizens, before concluding on the impact of Blair and Brown on the three key areas that the great decline debate really comes down to: political economy, global position and identity.

*

After the Treaty of Westphalia inaugurated the age of the nation state, relations between countries were governed by realpolitik considerations of power and force. In the nineteenth century, as Bismarck forged the German nation state through his wars against France and Austria, the parameters of the test of greatness of a nation were crystallised. By the twentieth century the test of a country's greatness seemed obvious: can it win wars? In Hitler's bid for world domination it reached its logical conclusion. This idea of greatness was best put into words by Stalin. The French politician Pierre Laval was trying to convince him to be more tolerant of religious minorities, especially Catholics. According to Winston Churchill's account, Stalin dismissed him with the question: 'The Pope! How many divisions has *he* got?'[20] Churchill's obvious admiration for the quip underlines the extent to which its wisdom was accepted by leaders while its lasting popularity shows the extent to which it articulated a common-sense view of how a state's greatness was measured. There was a simple formula for such measurements: to the level and sophistication of a state's technology was added its capacity for mass production. This sum was then multiplied by the amount of land ruled by the state and the number of people who called themselves citizens of that state. These products were then combined with the state's human military strength and financial reserves to form a measure of its greatness. This view of greatness was present at both the beginning and the end of the century.[21]

The twentieth century began with an arms race based on the size and strength of ships.[22] This race developed into a confrontation between major powers based around the fear of what the others would do. The systems created for the mobilisation of these huge and complex mechanised armies could be triggered by the actions of other states, creating a momentum which was unstoppable once a tipping point of crisis had been reached.[23] The result was the First World War. The middle and latter part of the century were dominated by another arms race. This time it was the size, number and power of missiles that most counted and it was the USA that was the superpower setting the terms of the race. The Cold War doctrine of 'mutually assured destruction' was summed up by John F. Kennedy's Secretary of Defense, Robert McNamara, in a famous speech of 1967:

> It is important to understand that assured destruction is the very essence of the whole deterrence concept. We must possess an actual assured-destruction capability, and that capability also must be credible. The point is that a potential aggressor must believe that our assured-destruction capability

is in fact actual, and that our will to use it in retaliation to an attack is in fact unwavering. The conclusion, then, is clear: if the United States is to deter a nuclear attack on itself or its allies, it must possess an actual and a credible assured-destruction capability.[24]

In both these arms races and in the final showdown with the Soviet Union in the mid-1980s, it was numbers, sizes, capacities and scales that defined the nature of greatness. Ronald Reagan's most important moves in the second phase of the Cold War had been based on an understanding – intuitive as much as evidence based – that the numbers the Soviets claimed were unsustainable if true and therefore probably false. In other words the historical bluff of the Stalinist state could be called;[25] it was; and the world changed.

The size of armies and the power of armaments were not the only measures of greatness that the nineteenth century had bequeathed the twentieth. After 1845, Jackson Democrats in the USA used the phrase 'manifest destiny' to describe and justify westward expansion at the expense of the Indian nations.[26] In *McClure's Magazine* in February 1899, Rudyard Kipling published his poem 'The White Man's Burden':

Take up the White Man's burden –
Send forth the best ye breed –
Go, bind your sons to exile
To serve your captives' need;
To wait, in heavy harness,
On fluttered folk and wild –
Your new-caught sullen peoples,
Half devil and half child.

Kipling's suggestion that the people of the colonies were 'half devil and half child' reflected a 'common-sense' notion of the Imperial Age that humanity was divided into races which had different attributes and stages of development. Moreover, these differences could be measured and quantified by physical characteristics. From a God-given notion of manifest destiny there developed a 'scientific' and 'rational' explanation for European dominance of the globe based on the idea of a hierarchy of races. These ideas extended through a misreading of Darwin into theories of normality and abnormality that called for the controlling of who within a given nation would be allowed by the state to reproduce. In 1933, when Hitler took power in Germany, race became the defining ideology of a major European state for the first time but racial theories of the division of humanity and eugenics-based concepts about normality had been mainstream ideas in European states for decades before. The racial make-up of the state added a further dimension to how a state's greatness might be measured but armies and empires remained the things to have and wars were the things to win. And the century saw many wars. Wars between states.

Until the First World War such wars had been fought over territory, trade and possessions. The Second World War added race and ethnicity to the list of causes for which millions could be butchered. In these competitions between states and in the ways in which these competitions were measured, Britain was a great power in a relative and in an absolute sense. It was economically great but no longer, as it had been in the nineteenth century, the single largest economy or the most important exporting nation.[27] Relative to other powers and in key sectors of the economy such as shipping, financial services and some aspects of manufacturing, it was a great power and in some areas, most notably financial services and banking, it was still the pre-eminent one.[28] Germany was rising, the USA manufacturing sector and primary and extractive industries gained ground every year[29] and in the distance more and more was being written about the force of Japan and its potential. When the First World War broke out Britain was doing better relative to these powers and to economic performance than in the last quarter of the nineteenth century, as measured by indicators such as economic growth. It was also absolutely a great power in that its naval force, the productive and human capacity of the empire, and the extent and solidity of its global financial holdings made it more capable than any other single power to wage total war. To an extent this was still the case in 1939. It was not only accident or bravado that made Churchill argue that Britain should fight on in 1940 – though both of these are parts of the equation. It was also the reality that ship for ship, plane for plane and life for life, Britain was more than matching the manufacturing output, financial reach and human sacrifice of the Third Reich as the war began.[30]

In his classic study, *England and the Aeroplane*, which demolished large sections of the declinist theories of Correlli Barnett,[31] David Edgerton lays out the case with respect to the most complex and effective weaponry of the Second World War: aeroplanes. He cites the study made by the engineer Eric Mensforth during the war itself. Mensforth compared the efficiency of the British aeroplane industry with that of the USA. He found that the US industry was 75 per cent more efficient, a figure much lower than that cited by Barnett and largely explained by the scale of production – it is just much more efficient to make larger numbers of aircraft. On a plane-by-plane, worker-by-worker basis, the efficiency was comparable. The really telling section of Edgerton's study concerns a comparison of Britain not with the USA but with the Third Reich. Edgerton argues that the great historian Richard Overy showed that the German aircraft industry was appallingly inefficient in the first years of the war. He suggests that in 1940 Britain and Germany devoted the same quantity of resources to aircraft production, while in terms of numbers Britain produced 50 per cent more. Between 1939 and 1941 the Germans doubled the resources they put into aircraft production, planning for an increase in output of between 200 per cent and 400 per cent: they produced 30 per cent more.

In 1944 Albert Speer took over, rationalised and increased the use of slave labour to produce a threefold increase. But by then the war was as good as lost.[32] In an absolute sense, then, in 1940 Britain was a great power among great powers.

This great power reality fed and was reflected in the place of racial ideology in the British political system. Such notions were strengthened by widespread circulation of the idea of a natural order of racial groupings used to explain British and European dominance of large sections of the planet. There was a strong strain of what the Nazis would have recognised as racial superiority, but outside some pockets of the imperial machine, the Sudan Political Service or the Indian Civil Service for example, it coexisted with a tradition of liberalism and evolving parliamentary democracy. Nor was any aspect of it eliminationalist, in the sense that British racial superiority or indeed British imperialism did not want to remove other races from the earth so much as make them all British. So this strain of racism was real, influential and at times dominant in policy-making decisions but it was not all-consuming. It is a cliché worth repeating that the essence of British imperialism was pragmatism. It was pragmatism that allowed the swift and relatively bloodless nature of our withdrawal from empire.

There was no Wagnerian dimension to the political nature of British racism, nor was there an Armageddon in which imperialism produced the destruction of the British state. There was nothing like the battle for Berlin or the years of near starvation that followed Germany's defeat in the Second World War. Therefore the nature of British racism was not confronted in the reconstruction of the British welfare state and society after 1945 nor, to an extent, in the creation of a new liberal society in the 1960s. Within this post-war concept of greatness and making up a significant element of the self-image of the state and the extent of its power, the idea of British racial superiority remained intact. The white British race was still held to be one of the great races of the world. Being white and British was seen as a privilege that carried with it responsibilities and burdens. In the second half of the twentieth century these ideas evolved and became much subtler, often unspoken and certainly routinely challenged. But they did not disappear.

Twice in the twentieth century, in 1914 and in 1939, the force of competition between states on these concrete and constructed measures of greatness took themselves and their empires into wars which spanned the globe: wars of unprecedented destruction. Sixty-two million people died in the Second World War. The powers that were competing for greatness in the twentieth century took very different approaches to the means by which they mobilised to fight these bloody conflicts. The nature of the regimes that fought in the First World War were different. Germany and Austria-Hungary used more coercion against their people in mobilising for war than did Britain and France, though the British and French were certainly not blameless in this regard.[33] The real contrast between the different political systems and the ways in which they waged war came in the Second World War, because it was part of an ideological civil war which was waged across Europe for much of the century and had its roots in the First World War but really commenced with the Bolshevik revolution in 1917. The first instalment of this civil war was therefore between democracy and communism. The challenge that communism represented to the democracies was that their working-class populations would abandon the parliamentary road in favour of a revolution. This was compounded by the stock market crash in 1929 and subsequent worldwide depression. With communism representing an extreme option for meeting the challenge of the depression on the left, there also developed extreme options on the right. In some ways these two options were mirror images. At their heart was the same attitude to individual citizens. For both communism and fascism, human beings were a means to an end and were expendable. Therefore when war began between these differing ideologies their approaches to human beings led them to pursue very different kinds of policies. Both used force but for the democracies there were limits to the force that could be used. For the Nazis and the communists there were no limits to the barbarity that would be deployed in the pursuit of victory.

In contrast to her opponents' barbarity, when Britain mobilised for total war the state had to make concessions to its people. In the First World War the deal was to extend civil and political rights to all citizens in exchange for their fighting. Such rights included giving women the vote and thereby finally bringing them into the definition of who the British 'political' nation were. This extension of rights also meant allowing socialist parties into government. It did not extend to the kind of social settlement that had been promised in the famous phrase of David Lloyd George – 'homes fit for heroes' – but it did include a new political settlement.

In the manner of the winning of the First World War and in the political settlement that flowed from it, the British state showed it had a significant capacity for including new or emerging groups in the process of political power. This is not to say that real power was spread by the elite willingly or, indeed, in meaningful ways without a struggle.[34] Once they were allowed into the circle of power, however, previously excluded groups were thereafter made to feel part of the political process. These inclusions were combined with some strokes of what can only be called good fortune. For example the relative softness of the impact of the interwar depression on the UK compared to other states was in part at least due to a certain amount of luck. The UK had developed new industries, with minimal state direction, in the south and the Midlands, in places where older industries had not flourished. The disproportionate impact of the depression on stable and traditional manufacturing concentrated its worst aspects geographically. This meant that there did not develop the same evenly spread group of disaffected voters from the lower middle class or the working class as developed in Germany, where the depression was sharper and the level of unemployment much higher in key years.

To think about the way in which the depression played out in terms of good fortune may seem strange. I stress it here because I want avoid the trap of implying that there was a predetermined path of exceptionalism that British history was following. The people running the British state made some good choices in the interwar years and the people creating companies in this period made rational judgements about where they should be placed. There were also some interesting features of the way in which the British political system worked in comparison with the political systems of other states. But there was nothing inevitable about the survival of British democracy and little embedded in British culture that made it more able to survive. A culture is not set on a course by its history; rather its history shapes and determines the meaning, content and dimensions of that culture. The vital point is that, for whatever reason or combination of reasons, British democracy survived in the interwar years. The left did not exit democracy in favour of revolution and dictatorship on the model of the Soviet Union. The right did not exit democracy in favour of a strong government to protect capital on the model of Italy or Germany. This survival of democracy in Britain between 1918 and 1945 was the first remarkable illustration of the flexibility and adaptability of the twentieth-century British state and its political system. But it was not the last. It was a dynamism derived from the force of consensus and the power of inclusion as a counterweight to polarisation. It was a dynamism born of the accident of human capital in the shape of the political leaders who dominated the scene in these years.

In the Second World War the scale and the nature of the destruction of total war required a deeper compact or settlement between the governed and the government. Social and economic power was to be distributed through welfare states for the benefit of the people. This deal, struck in the reconstruction committees which met even as the fighting was going on, was enacted as Britain was rebuilt and it was augmented by the retreat from empire in the gradual process of decolonisation. British politics came home in a prolonged rearguard action. This was not achieved without cost. Terrible atrocities were committed in many places by the British as they exited and because they exited. But it was better than the exit strategies of other European empires and was achieved more quickly.

The decolonisation of the British Empire was the second great adaptive episode of the dynamic British state in the post-war period. In the process of changing from Empire to Commonwealth, the white state became the multinational and multicultural state. The experience of black and Asian citizens who came from the periphery of empire to the centre was, of course, mixed and often negative. The way in which the state dealt with the new constructions of multicultural communities was again based on the pursuit of inclusion and the forging of consensus. The success of the British model of multiculturalism was as imperfect as the success of the political and economic policies of the interwar period but in the post-war period, as in the interwar period, the major challenges were dealt with remarkably well, especially in the 1950s. The running of British political economy was based after 1945 on a progressive consensus forged by the post-war Attlee government which enshrined full employment as the primary political objective of the state. It was full employment which underpinned the operation of the British model of multiculturalism. One could argue that the model lasted exactly as long as full employment lasted.[35]

The crucial lesson the democracies learnt from the 1930s was that high unemployment could destroy them.[36] The Bretton Woods system and the operation of Keynesian demand management maintained the welfare state and full employment down to the mid-1970s. In this thirty-year period the test of a nation's greatness evolved in new ways. Western European states sheltering under the American nuclear umbrella and defended by the American garrisons in West Germany switched from measuring their greatness by the number of their tanks to competing for the lowest unemployment rate and the highest rate of growth. Underpinning economic growth and full employment was a welfare system based on universal provision. European states began to gradually lose their dominance of the world manufacturing sectors and concentrate more on information and services, but the jobs stayed intact, defended by the trade union movement. In much of Europe this developed into the social market economy that enshrined tripartism and a developmental state at the heart of the political economy.

Britain took a slightly different route, with more limited scope for tripartism because of the way in which the public sector was organised. However, across Europe, including Britain, affluence produced unprecedented access to leisure and recreation.

This affluence was expressed in a particular way in Britain in an explosion of creativity in the 1960s – sponsored in no small part by Labour and Conservative governments interested and engaged in the promoting the arts. Leisure produced many of its own problems and challenges but it did not promote, as mass unemployment in the 1930s had done, widespread exiting from democracy. The alienation of the young generated by affluence and the problems of relative deprivation that dominated debate in the 1960s were both the kinds of problem that the leaders of the 1930s and the 1970s would have been happy to cope with. But affluence also led to challenges to the unity of the nation state as Northern Irish Catholics and a minority of Scottish and Welsh citizens felt that they were not enjoying the civil and political rights or the economic progress they should be. These discontents were to turn increasingly violent in the 1970s. There were further dark sides to this affluence in the 1960s. The long boom that maintained peace between Western nation states was sustained by the creation of a permanent underclass excluded from the benefits of peace and while the Europeans did not fight each other, they exported war.

The nature of a society that encourages the existence of an underclass providing the basis for the affluence of the long boom is best described in the title of J. K. Galbraith's 1992 study, *The Culture of Contentment*. Galbraith's argument was that Western states were divided between a contented class who enjoyed a stable level of affluence and voted accordingly, an insecure class who slipped in and out of safe comfort and an underclass who lived a life of insecurity in both a material and often a physical sense. This underclass remains a feature of contemporary Britain.[37]

The affluence of the long boom rested on the existence of the underclass; peace rested on the exportation of war. The Cold War generated almost endless hostilities outside Europe: wars of national liberation that featured bloody counter-insurgencies, such as the fight against the Mau Mau in Kenya or the French struggle to cling to Algeria; proxy wars fought out between the USA and the Soviet Union in third countries, like the long and awful conflict in Angola; wars resulting from the botched nature of the decolonisation process, such as the series of conflicts and confrontations between India and Pakistan. But in western Europe and in the United Kingdom, outside the province of Ulster, the period from the late 1940s to the early 1970s was one of extraordinary stability, peace and progress. You would never believe this from the numerous histories that were written during and immediately after the long boom.

When the OPEC states raised the price of oil in the early 1970s the structural problems of the post-war economic system were exposed. The shock of the oil crisis contributed to the collapse of Bretton Woods and the undermining of the validity of the policy of Keynesian demand management. In the face of rising oil prices and increased world competition the post-war boom ended, the stability of the era of full employment was shattered, and the peace was destroyed as violence in Ulster became institutionalised and seemingly permanent.

The different orientations between Britain and the other states of Europe were now more starkly exposed as different policy responses emerged to the stagflation of the 1970s. The Europeans dug in deeper to the social market economies, resting on the social market 'Rhine' model and hoping that deeper integration would ensure that good levels of growth could be sustained. In contrast, within a decade of the first oil shock, the UK was pursuing an Atlantic capitalist response. Under Margaret Thatcher's governments a radical and dynamic response to a crisis was adopted. These policies were based on deregulation, tax cutting and privatisation. The Attlee compact, which had promised full employment and universal welfare, was broken and Britain adopted even more strongly a political economy that looked like Galbraith's *Culture of Contentment* – an acceptance of high levels of unemployment, increasing poverty and alienation and increasing gaps between rich and poor. The hope was that the restructuring of British industry further away from manufacturing towards the knowledge economy would restore competitiveness and eventually reduce unemployment. This set of policies was accompanied by a resurgence of race-dominated language of nationalism and a turning back on the philosophy of universal welfare provision and full employment. British people seemed to question the nature of the multicultural society that the waves of immigration in the 1950s and 1960s had created in many towns. Brixton, Toxteth and Southall burned while Norman Tebbit introduced his test of loyalty by asking which team first- and second-generation immigrants supported at cricket. After eighteen years of Thatcherite economic management the basic restructuring and reconstruction of Britain's economy had been achieved but at the cost of increasing the size of the permanent underclass who were excluded from the benefits of contentment. Then New Labour was elected and a new century dawned.

3

Consensus and beyond

If we accept the broad shape of this overview of Britain in the twentieth century then a chronological framework follows from it and, at least for the period since 1945, it makes sense to view the construction of this chronology through the prism of the operation of or challenge to consensus. By consensus I do not mean that there was agreement between the major parties on everything. Much of the critique of the traditional consensus view of British politics attacked and unsurprisingly demolished this straw person view by finding things on which the two parties disagreed and claiming that this proved there was no such thing as consensus.[1] Consensus is the ideological foundation of British politics, the working parameters within which it operated, the locus of what was thought open to change, what the prevailing political common sense accepted as a settled way of doing things. I am not suggesting here that politicians necessarily agreed with that way of doing things – that Conservatives embraced nationalised industries or that Labourites endorsed privatisation. They made a judgement about what was politically possible and electorally tolerable. They might have been wrong about these judgements but what constrained Conservatives from embarking on widespread privatisation in 1951 and Labour from embarking on widespread nationalisation in 1997 is what I mean by consensus.

A simple schema of the periodisation of the post-war years looks something like this:

1943–50	The formation of the Attlee consensus[2]
1950–9	The Attlee consensus in operation
1959–79	The challenge to and breakdown of the Attlee consensus and a developing sense of political instability
1979–92	Non-consensus politics ending in consensus formation
1992–2003	The Thatcher consensus in operation, evolving into the Blair–Brown consensus after 1997
2003–7	Consensus in operation but with ever-increasing challenges

The first phase was the construction of the consensus. This began at the point at which reconstruction began to be considered, after the victory at Stalingrad in 1943, and continued until after the main body of Labour's legislative programme and the major structures of the Cold War had been established, around 1949–50. Once the consensus had been constructed it then operated effectively for a relatively short period, from 1949 until around the time of the 1959 election. There were two major challenges to the operation of the consensus in this period – Suez and an ongoing debate about the status of sterling in the world economy. Suez caused a massive trauma about Britain's relative position but it did not alter or challenge other elements in the operation of the consensus. The pound inspired the first major work in the decline debate, Andrew Shonfield's analysis of the position of the currency, published in 1958.[3]

It took several years for the debate to gather steam, but by 1959–60 the consensus was being assaulted from both left and right, in political analysis and cultural commentary, as Britain's problems appeared to be building up. The economy began to slow and Britain's position in the world became more uncertain. The period 1959–79 saw the slow break-down of the consensus on how the British state should be run, on the meaning of British identity and what Britain's position in the world should be. The Attlee settlement was beginning to be attacked from the left and the right and British world power became increasingly uncertain. In turn the best geopolitical strategy for Britain to pursue became unclear. It was in this period that immigration first began to expose the myths upon which the idea of a monocultural and tolerant Britain rested. At the same time the long boom ended and British manufacturing appeared vulnerable and full employment unsustainable. In these years the decline debate was a national conversation. This conversation or argument was generated by objective reality; it was not all imagined. In the period of the breaking down of the consensus there were three broad areas of problems faced by Britain: problems of political economy, problems of global status and problems of identity. Each of these problems generated debates and positions that were more or less programmatic; that is, they suggested ways in which the problems identified could be resolved. Indeed, the Conservative Party's actual programme in 1970 and the Labour Party's manifesto in 1974 offered starkly different policies.

At the end of this prolonged period of ideological instability, the debate was simplified to being for or against Thatcherism. In the ensuing period, 1979–92, the consensus did not operate. The number of major areas of British politics and culture that were profoundly contested outweighed those on which there was a broad agreement or at least a dominant view, which appeared at the time to be hegemonic. The idea that suggesting radical alternatives or diametrically opposed sets of policies would be electorally costly was jettisoned.

The era of non- or even anti-consensus politics lasted until after the 1992 election. There then began the construction of a new consensus based on the broad parameters of the Thatcher settlement, the assumptions of which were then translated into a conventional wisdom on what was electorally doable. It is difficult to date this new consensus before 1992 because Labour remained committed to withdrawal from the European Community, unilateral nuclear disarmament, increasing direct taxation to fund public expenditure and renationalisation of a gradually reducing list of industries. The initial shifts signalled in the 1992 election were stabilised by 1997 with the positive embrace of the market economy, the European Union (as it had by then become known) and even nuclear weapons. This substantially altered the nature of the consensus by placing the public sector and public services at the centre of the debate. From 1997 to 2003 the Blair–Brown consensus, built on the foundations of the Thatcher settlement, operated successfully; after 2003 it entered a period of uncertainty but it remains the case that any Conservative government elected in the near future will operate very much within the terms of reference established by the Blair–Brown governments, much as the Conservative governments elected after 1951 operated within the terms of the Attlee consensus.

The construction and deconstruction of the consensus is in part based on the synthesis of different positions. The thesis presented by the centre and right of British politics in response to the crisis in political economy in the interwar period was based on a traditional response of minimal state intervention and deflation. This provoked an antithesis from the left based on the ownership of industry, control of prices and reflation. The war forced a synthesis of these positions, which was articulated in the legislative programme of the Attlee governments and solidified by the Conservatives' failure to reverse that programme in 1951. Clement Attlee's legislative programme was based on a modernising agenda which put forward the broadly accepted norms of the day. In 1979 Margaret Thatcher was not synthesising an accepted set of beliefs about the best policy solutions to the problems of the day; rather she was proposing a radical thesis about what should be changed. This programme was not synthesised until the Blair–Brown governments were elected. In the period before consensus operation, Thatcher was pursuing a modernisation project in many ways even more audacious than the Attlee programme, because when she began her programme of reform, she was taking the lead in advocating deregulation and privatisation as a response to the crisis of the late 1970s. All other European countries were still wedded to the idea that the Rhine model could be made to work. The Attlee collectivist project was part of a Europe-wide move towards greater state intervention. The legislative record of the Blair–Brown governments has often been dismissed in comparison to the Attlee and Thatcher projects because it lacked substance. This conclusion is true if you see these projects through the lenses of the state and judge these outcomes in terms of the rearrangement of social furniture on a grand scale. What Blair–Brown has done is much less dramatic but if you look at it from the perspective of the citizen it appears more sustainable and appropriate in the context of the age we live in as a way of doing politics.

Seeing like a citizen: the dynamic British state and its peoples

The major argument against the positive analysis of the Blair–Brown governments from the centre-left is based around a critique of their way of governing rather than any particular set of decisions they have made or failed to make. Many writers who are critical of the Blair–Brown governments argue that the operation of Cabinet government has been replaced by an over-powerful Prime Minister, that the executive is more powerful than the legislature and that the atmosphere of Westminster and Whitehall is dominated by competition between secretive cliques.[4] Rules on party finance may have been broken if not in the letter of the law then certainly in its spirit. What has been replaced by the New Labour way of doing business is often called civil society, the institutions that exist between the individual citizen and the power of the state. Civil society in this argument is the form of government that writers particularly favoured at any one time. A social democratic government with a small parliamentary majority, such as Wilson's and Callaghan's between 1974 and 1979, had by necessity to govern through Parliament but Thatcher's and then Blair's majorities significantly reduced Parliament's centrality. Did this reduction therefore destroy civil society? It certainly changed the way business was done, but civil society is not actually about how business is done. Civil society is what protects citizens from the state, it is the intermediate institutions. The reality of post-war British history is that citizens were not protected by civil society institutions against strong modernising projects; on the contrary, these produced victims in a way that the statecraft and political economy of Blair–Brown – for good or ill – have not.

The arrival of New Labour in 1997 heralded the beginning of a new modernisation project. Tony Blair's introduction to the 1997 manifesto made clear that the new 'project' was going to build on and not reverse the Thatcher revolution:

> I believe in Britain. It is a great country with a great history. The British people are a great people. But I believe Britain can and must be better: better schools, better hospitals, better

ways of tackling crime, of building a modern welfare state, of equipping ourselves for a new world economy.

I want a Britain that is one nation, with shared values and purpose, where merit comes before privilege; run for the many not the few, strong and sure of itself at home and abroad.

I want a Britain that does not shuffle into the new millennium afraid of the future, but strides into it with confidence.

I want to renew our country's faith in the ability of its government and politics to deliver this new Britain. I want to do it by making a limited set of important promises and achieving them. This is the purpose of the bond of trust I set out at the end of this introduction, in which ten specific commitments are put before you. Hold us to them. They are our covenant with you.

I want to renew faith in politics by being honest about the last 18 years. Some things the Conservatives got right. We will not change them. It is where they got things wrong that we will make change. We have no intention or desire to replace one set of dogmas by another.

I want to renew faith in politics through a government that will govern in the interest of the many, the broad majority of people who work hard, play by the rules, pay their dues and feel let down by a political system that gives the breaks to the few, to an elite at the top increasingly out of touch with the rest of us.

And I want, above all, to govern in a way that brings our country together, that unites our nation in facing the tough and dangerous challenges of the new economy and changed society in which we must live. I want a Britain which we all feel part of, in whose future we all have a stake, in which what I want for my own children I want for yours.

Blair's project, as emotively articulated here, was therefore to modernise Britain. In considering the Blair project as an attempt to achieve radical change we need to compare it with previous modernisation projects. Was this to be as ambitious a set of reforms as had occurred before? What was the nature of New Labour's modernisation project in comparison to previous projects?

The notion of modernising a country is itself problematic. A country is not like a house or even a city. Politics is not like DIY. It is extremely difficult to manage the expectations of voters when you set out to promise change. The very notion of undertaking 'modernisation' can be questioned both when the blueprints for a new order are produced and as the policies are being translated into reality. Even the most successful modernisation projects of British political history only partially fulfilled what they had promised. When the ideology of the New Right began to be put into practice after 1979 its success was only limited. The New Right assaults on the operation of the public sector, the universal basis for welfare provision and the very existence of the state coexisted with forms of intervention in social and cultural policy and in defence which were based on the successful operation of state power. Moreover, resistance to substantial cutbacks in the basis of welfare payments or restrictions on the length of time that relief could be offered effectively stopped the Thatcher revolution in its tracks.

The self-confidence of the project, as it was over-whelmingly demonstrated in its deregulation policies and privatisation programmes, tends to be written about more than the compromises. This sense of self-confidence and belief was also very clearly working on the left as well during the Attlee years and was expressed through the need to compromise with the private sector and negotiate change with professional groups such as doctors. Nevertheless the

Attlee and the Thatcher projects are both seen as substantially more wide-ranging and successful than the Blair–Brown projects have been. Rather than interpreting this as the political failure of New Labour in power, however, it is also possible to construct a defence of the limited ambition of the Blair–Brown projects in comparison with the earlier modernisation projects by exploring the work of James C. Scott.

In *Seeing like a State*[5] Scott explores the failure of a range of modernisation projects from the high modernism of Lenin, as it set out to transform a society through revolution, to schemes for planning and building model cities. He asks himself why 'so many well-intended schemes to improve the human condition have gone so tragically awry'. He suggests that these projects were embarked upon because of a combination of four factors:

1. The administrative ordering of nature and society – the things the state does to make society legible and ultimately governable.
2. The arrogant assumptions embedded in high-modernist ideology about the possibility of a science of society and politics.
3. When the mechanism of governance is combined with the will to govern created by high modernism, you have a potentially lethal combination in the authoritarian state.
4. In turn this shrinks civil society to such an extent that the intermediaries between the state and the citizen are removed.

Scott summarises these conditions thus: 'The legibility of a society provides the capacity for large-scale social engineering, high-modernist ideology provides the desire, the authoritarian state provides the determination to act on that desire, and an incapacitated civil society provides the levelled social terrain on which to build.'[6] Once launched these projects fail, according to Scott, because the modernisers 'regarded themselves as far smarter and farseeing than they really were, and at the same time, regarded their subjects as far more stupid and incompetent than they really were'.[7] In particular, Scott claims, the high modernists tried to replace 'organic' patterns of organisation with rationalised ones:

> In each case, the necessarily thin, schematic model of social organisation and production animating the planning was inadequate as a set of instructions for creating a successful social order. By themselves, the simplified rules can never generate a functioning community, city, or economy. Formal order, to be more explicit, is always and to some degree parasitic on informal processes, which the formal scheme does not recognize, without which it could not exist, and which it alone cannot create or maintain.[8]

As Scott's argument demonstrates, by ignoring the informal arrangements that underpin social intercourse, by replacing local knowledge and expertise with abstract theory and by ignoring the existing shape and texture of society, the modernisers failed. Despite this failure Scott retains a feeling for the motivation of the planners and criticises those who reject the possibility of modernisation:

> What conservatives like Oakeshott miss, I think, is that high modernism has a natural appeal for an intelligentsia and a people who may have ample reason to hold the past in contempt. Revolutionaries have had every reason to despise the feudal, poverty-stricken, inegalitarian past that they hoped to banish forever, and sometimes they have also had a

reason to suspect that immediate democracy would simply bring back the old order. Post-independence leaders in the non-industrial world (occasionally revolutionary leaders themselves) could not be faulted for hating their past of colonial domination and economic stagnation, nor could they be faulted for wasting no time or democratic sentimentality on creating a people that they could be proud of. Understanding the history and logic of their commitment to high-modernist goals, however, does not permit us to overlook the enormous damage that their convictions entailed when combined with authoritarian state power.[9]

I think the really telling phrase here is 'nor could they be faulted for wasting no time or democratic sentimentality on creating a people that they could be proud of'. Scott does not consider modernisation projects instigated by liberal democracies. Though his work is infused with a compassion for the victims of modernising projects, Scott is not concerned with considering the experience of schemes to improve the human condition from the perspective of the human being to be improved.

British politics in the twenty-first century could not operate in the way in which Scott suggests previous modernisation projects have worked. In terms of the Blair–Brown governments, critics make two contradictory accusations. In one set of attacks the Blair–Brown governments lack any ideological confidence and therefore their political approach is timid and weak. In the second set the Blair–Brown governments are led by arrogant and power-obsessed control freaks who fail to take any account of the opinions of those who are the victims of their policies. Both of these things cannot of course be true but elements of both of them combined do suggest the basis of Blair–Brown's statecraft, which is both consultative and assertive. To understand this combination we need to consider the way in which modernisation is thought of and the way in which the Attlee and Thatcher projects operated.

In considering modernisation, I reject both the notion that only left-progressive political projects can be seen as modernising and the idea that modernisation is by definition something inherently good and synonymous with human advancement. We need to be conscious of the value judgements we bring to the assessment of the success or failure of a particular project. To put it very crudely: there are good regimes and bad regimes; there are good governments and bad governments. Often this implicit value system is graded, moving from the uncontested to the contested something like this:

Uncontested bad	Right-wing totalitarian regimes
	Left-wing totalitarian regimes
	Monarchical authoritarian regimes
	Republican authoritarian regimes
Contested	Partial democracies based on land ownership
	Partial democracies based on property
	Partial democracies based on gender
Uncontested good	Universal suffrage

This 'grading' of governments extends into the 'grading' of victims. Political projects launched by governments of the left and right in any one of these different regimes are in their different ways trying to create a perfect citizen. That perfect citizen might be created by enslaving large numbers of other citizens, indeed, by denying their right to citizenship because of their race (Hitler's war against the Jews) or class (Stalin's mass murder of richer peasants or kulaks); or the perfect citizen might be created by a project of mass education and social housing (Attlee's Britain) or deregulation and encouraging enterprise (Thatcher's Britain). All these kinds of project can be born of the set of factors Scott describes as necessary for large-scale projects to be launched, and they all create victims. Because of such grading of political regimes we frequently see an unequal regard for their victims and even at times a failure to recognise that some kinds of reform produce victims at all, a view that exists in much of the writing about Attlee's nationalisation project, as I argue further below. The really telling point to take from Scott's analysis is the assumption that projects for creating such a 'socialised society' or an 'enterprise culture' can be done amid the disregard for the needs or desires of the 'victims' of the project.

In exploring the lives and careers of a number of social democratic politicians over the last ten years or so, I have very rarely encountered in the speeches, letters or diaries of my subjects the form of self-doubt that says: do people actually want this? The kinds of politician I have been writing about have tended to assume – some, such as Aneurin Bevan,[10] with considerable justification, some, such as Woodrow Wyatt,[11] with none – that they had a special kind of insight into what their natural constituency wanted. They all, with the exception of Gordon Brown,[12] shared a dislike or indifference to the contemporary paraphernalia of focus groups, policy option testing, opinion polling and deliberative policy formation. Even Brown, though relaxed with the use of these techniques, is an old-fashioned politician in that he has a working model for the way the world should be and is striving to move it in that direction. He hopes that the electorate will follow; he is not following the electorate. My earlier subjects, Hugh Gaitskell and Ernest Bevin in particular,[13] clearly felt comfortable with the notion that they knew what was best for the people and Anthony Crosland clearly thought that he knew or that the people of Grimsby would tell him when he was very wrong.[14] Each of these politicians was part of a democratic project to change people's minds, to make them better social democrats and, ultimately for most of them, with the possible exception of Wyatt and Desmond Donnelly,[15] to make them 'better people'.

In believing in these things this group of democratic socialists and social democrats was part of the five main democratic socialist modernising projects of the post-Second World War era:

1. the nationalisation programme of the 1945–51 government
2. the housing and town planning programme of the 1940s–1960s
3. the creation of comprehensive education
4. the expansion of the welfare state
5. the creation of the National Health Service.

The first two of these projects were almost unmitigated disasters in terms of the long-stated reasons for doing them. The first promised to socialise society and failed to do so. The second, with some localised exceptions, destroyed communities the length and breadth of the UK without consulting people and with little regard for the social or cultural consequences. The final three achieved much more of what they set out to achieve and are therefore more easily defensible in terms of their impact on people's lives. Nevertheless, they were also created against the strong opposition of many stakeholders. Welfare, health and education policy have also had mixed results, not least because of the fundamental lack of political will on the part of the British left since the war to see the process of reform as being based, in David Marquand's phrase, on a developmental state.[16] The five modernising projects, taken together, formed the high tide of democratic socialism; they became the settlement of the New Jerusalem rather than its beginning. From the perspective of the citizens whose minds and lives were to be changed the impact was mixed but the lesson clear: in all these schemes 'metis', local knowledge and consent, were largely irrelevant to the modernisers.

The response to these projects came in the 1980s in a series of equally ambitious modernising projects instigated by Conservative governments elected after 1979:

1. privatisation of state-owned industries
2. regulation of trade unions
3. sale of council houses
4. market deregulation.

The purpose of this programme of reform was to create an enterprise culture and a free market. The privatisation was carried out with little consultation and in the case of the trade unions, with the overt intention of destroying existing relations in order to change mindsets throughout industry. The result was the transformation of the British economy. Where once there was a mixed economy in which manufacturing, and the social architecture associated with it, played a significant role and in which there was a substantial stock of public housing, now there is an economy in which service industries dominate and social structures are significantly less stable. From the perspective of the citizens whose lives were changed the impact was mixed but the lesson clear: in all these schemes metis, local knowledge and consent were largely irrelevant to the modernisers.

In the social democratic and neo-liberal projects of modernisation we see the same basic failure of communication and consultation in the framing and implementation of policy. It is banal to say that this is the root of the problem in contemporary politics but even if it is banal, it is also true. And it has consequences for the way in which we view the use of focus groups and polling by contemporary political parties. In short, rather than despising these things we need our politicians to learn how to do them better.

To flesh out this argument I want to explore two of these dynamic political projects, which are intimately related: nationalisation and privatisation. Very simply, the most compelling reason why the political process that created and ran the nationalised industries failed as it did is the manner of their privatisation. The nationalisation programme of the post-war Labour government was planned, run and carried out in the context of a fully functioning civil society. The victims of these projects, the workers in the industries, the customers for the goods and services and the owners, did not perish – and I am not equating them as victims to the victims of the totalitarian modernisation projects that James C. Scott considers in his book. But that does not mean that they did not suffer in both an actual and a 'latent' sense, and it does not mean that there are not rankings within the realms of victims of democratic politics.

By latent suffering I mean the concealed disappointment felt by those who experienced the failings of these modernising projects. This disappointment developed over the post-war period, in the case of the Attlee settlement, into a significant constituency of 'natural' Labour supporters becoming Labour's opponents. The gap between the promise and the reality of Labour's modernising project in the 1940s created a sense of disappointment, a collapse in enthusiasm for the Labour movement. For the customers of these industries, latent disappointment describes the pleasure or satisfaction forgone because of the level of service or disservice provided by monopoly nationalised industries. For the former owners of nationalised industries, the suffering was real in the sense of a way of life that ended. Theirs might have been a way of life that lacked the romance and the literature of working-class life in a place like the Gorbals in Glasgow before modernisation came to clear the slums, but it was their way of life and in some cases had been for as many generations as there had been mines. I do not particularly want to privilege the sense of suffering of mine owners because of a possible future forgone, but neither do I think it is right merely to ignore it or dismiss it with reference to the payment of compensation. Do we credit redundancy pay as a valid form of recognition of the change in a life when a miner is paid off never to go down a pit again?

From the late 1930s onwards the idea of common owner-ship was constructed in Labour thinking as a vital tool for transforming society. No one in the Labour movement, not even Ernest Bevin and Aneurin Bevan, actually thought about how, in reality, altering the form of the ownership of industry would create the socialist utopia – the New Jerusalem. Labour's emphasis on the question of ownership was in fact almost entirely divorced from and frequently discussed separately from the kind of society that would exist and the kind of people who would live and work in that society. Indeed, the notion of a new society is gradually air-brushed out of Labour thinking. If you compare Ramsay MacDonald's *Socialism: Critical and Constructive* of 1921 with the essays in the second volume of Herbert Tracey's history of the first fifty years of the Labour Party,[17] what is striking is the way which the process of socialisation has become separated from the kind of society that will be created by nationalisation. MacDonald talks of the creation of communal property as the means to better motivate society and change the basis upon which people live:

> Here the socialist can lay down one of the foundation stones of his reconstructed society. The personal enjoyment of property possible to the mass of people from collective and not from individual ownership . . . Communal property, however, whilst enlivening the communal interests of the individual and enabling him to understand what community means and how its well-being is his own well-being, is not a sufficient motive for industry. It belongs to a better class of motive than the purely personal one, and we may hope that in time that class will be predominant.[18]

What was needed to achieve this change in people's values went beyond communal ownership towards what MacDonald called socialist incentives, by which he means control: 'the complete organisation of industry'. The point of the organisation of industry is to change society, in part at least by giving 'the workmen responsibility for the workshop'.[19] By 1948, Herbert Morrison is defending the record of the form of socialisation that has taken place thus: 'The essential aims are better public service, greater efficiency and economy, and the well-being and dignity of the workers employed in the industry or service.'[20] Between 1921 and 1948 MacDonald's insight seems to have been forgotten and there is no mention by Morrison of workers' control and no link to the creation of a new society. Instead there is the aim of running the industries better as industries, in other words industrial rather than social modernisation.

This break between society and industry was to have a devastating impact on how the notion of public ownership was received among the generation that came of age in the 1950s. In theory the creation of the public sector had produced the new society but in reality the first socialised generation rejected the notion that a mere change in formal ownership of a set of natural monopolies represented the creation of a new society. It quickly became apparent after 1947–8 that for most people, including large numbers of people working in the industries themselves, nationalisation had nothing to do with them. They were not victims of it as such, but neither were they part of it or it so much part of their lives that their values had been altered. For the British working class, life had not been changed, merely organisational structures altered.

But, like privatisation in the 1980s, nationalisation in the 1940s also had its victims. Can we compare the owners of industries that were nationalised by the Labour governments of 1945–51 and the miner of the 1980s? Both had their ways of life destroyed by a state-run democratic modernisation project that rejected local and specialist knowledge in favour of abstract political notions of how something should be done. Both were stigmatised, as being arch-reactionary opponents of the inevitable wave of the future, clinging to the wreckage of the past because they said that the policy the government of the day had embarked on could not work. What is the difference? The difference is again that you cannot join the club of the victims unless you are from a politically designated victim group. There are no property-owning victims in the vast bulk of historical and political science writing because ownership of property disbars them from being a victim. Or perhaps because progressive politics has no victims? Owners of that property, often truly awful and corrupt people, especially mine owners, are therefore made the scapegoats, not the victims – the evil plutocrats, another species who do not enjoy the same rights as workers; in Bevan's phrase, 'lower than vermin'.

The failure of nationalisation as a modernising project in its own terms is largely due to the exclusion of the main subjects of the modernisation, namely workers, from the process of running the industries. In a similar way the model adopted for privatisation by the Thatcher governments meant that the objective of creating a property-owning and entrepreneurial society was not significantly advanced by the selling of shares in nationalised industries. The bulk of the shares in the newly privatised companies such as British Telecom quickly transferred to existing large-scale share owners and though there was a net increase in share owner-ship this did not impact on the culture of the workforce in the industries privatised. While reform of union control and work place practices did change the culture of some of these industries, the basic mistake in privatisation was exactly the same as the basic mistake in nationalisation: the exclusion of the workforce from the process. A model akin to the John Lewis Partnership or the cooperative movement with dividend payment and share ownership might have been more successful in altering workers' perceptions with respect to property, or it might not. The point is that the workers in the nationalised industries did not need to be included in the process of privatisation because the form of nationalisation had not included them in the first place.

Is there an aspect of nationalisation that actually worked? In the age of the public ownership of industries, between 1945 and 1979, workers did not control their industries, they did not share in the full fruits of their labour, and the division between them and management gradually deepened. But more than this, society as expressed in dominant attitudes and behaviours remained essentially capitalist in orientation and was not socialised. The depth of the failure of nationalisation as a society-changing project needs to be seen in the context of what was expected of that nationalisation by the left. As early as the first half of the 1950s, Anthony Crosland, Hugh Gaitskell and Bevan all lamented the extent of the failure that had taken place. Bevan grapples with the problem in *In Place of Fear*, Crosland in the articles that led to *The Future of Socialism* and Gaitskell in his diary.[21] Mainly, however, the Labour Party skirted around Morrison's failure; indeed, if you attacked nationalisation from the social democratic right you were called a 'reactionary', while if you attacked it from the left you were revolutionary. Overall, the programme must go down as one of the greatest failures of imagination, honesty and courage in British political history. In government the Labour Party never attempted to democratise a single industry by spreading ownership in a genuinely participatory way or instituting localised workers' control on a cooperative basis. The general level of over-employment in the nationalised sector and the defence of differentials would not do as a substitute for a new society. Morrison acknowledged the need to develop the form of public ownership but all post-war policy making in this area was actually devoted to the format for bringing additional industries into public ownership rather than for reforming those that had been nationalised between 1945 and 1951. In commenting on Labour's performance in social policy over the twentieth century, Nick Ellison has written:

> Having realised a good many of their welfare objectives, as these had been understood by 1945, Labour governments did not manage to build on these foundations in the second half of the century. Instead, in retrograde fashion, they defended their creation without seeking substantially to improve it and certainly without critically examining the collectivist nature of welfare provision itself.[22]

Exactly the same could be said of nationalisation. The failure to actually transform attitudes and relationships through it was the key to the ability of the Conservative governments to privatise the nationalised industries. In only one industry was there a substantial confrontation: mining.

Mining was different not because the nature of the nationalisation was different, but because initially, of all the industries nationalised, it was the one in which the workers felt most triumphant. Though this feeling did not last, a certain sense of ownership did. We need, however, to be very careful when we consider the nature of ownership of the mines expressed by the National Union of Mineworkers (NUM). Nationalisation had not made the coal industry the miners' industry. The political analysis of miners' leaders such as Frank Cousins and Arthur Scargill was that the National Coal Board was as much the enemy as the state and capitalism. It meant that the NUM became a major political player in confrontations with Conservative governments. It was this political analysis which made the mining industry the scene of the major confrontation over privatisation during its year-long strike.

The destruction of the UK mining industry was not a necessary precondition for the neo-liberal modernisation of the British economy. Market deregulation did not require the creation of internal enemies. The unions were not too powerful to be controlled by the right laws. No matter what it felt like at the time, the state was not going to be destroyed by Arthur Scargill – as much as it suited Scargill and Margaret Thatcher to pretend otherwise. Indeed, it felt like that because it was made to feel like that, by the media, the government and the unions, to justify the political violence on both sides. The Thatcherite manifestation of the neo-liberal modernisation project required enemies who were to be made into victims as a necessary condition of the project. For Thatcher to modernise there needed to be a reactionary past to transcend, a conservative present to defeat, because the objective of Thatcherism was to destroy a mindset.

Democratic political projects have victims, but not by definition, because they are not designed around or based on the destruction of victims in order to fulfil the terms of their success in the way that totalitarian projects are. People retain a degree of choice in democracy and civil society – law, especially, exists as a buffer between state and individual. There are winners in democratic modernisation projects, there were winners from the Attlee settlement, especially in terms of access to health care, and there were winners in the Thatcher reforms, especially higher-rate taxpayers. The instigators and the subjects of democratic modernisation projects are not by definition victims. They become victims when their projects are designed and implemented in ways that disregard the need to mobilise and include. It has to be said that in UK democracy since 1945 this has been more often the case than not. Finally, the intentions of the modernisers make no difference. When projects fail people they create victims and it makes no difference to the modernised if the modernisers wanted to create a New Jerusalem or a new enterprise culture.

There is a requirement – a moral imperative – to understand the individual implications of political projects of modernisation. We need to construct politics from the victims up as it were, if we want to avoid the mistakes of the past – an issue I discuss later with respect to foreign policy. The Labour governments first elected in 1997 grasped in their approach to central political questions that the entire notion of political projects that set out to change minds from the top down has been discredited. It has been rejected in advanced industrial countries by increasing numbers of voters who stay at home or vote for extremes. Instead the Blair–Brown governments embraced a new kind of political project which accepted the constraints of the times and the limits of what people wanted, that lacked ambition about what could be changed but expressed a willingness to engage, at least in the earlier phase of the government to 2003, with stakeholders in the areas they were trying to reform, such as health and education.

To compare the modernisation project of the Blair–Brown governments with their predecessors' requires an acknowledgement that the context has significantly changed from both 1945 and 1979. Many commentators who write about New Labour were born and brought up in a world in which choice was not central to individual identity and therefore the relationship between voter and politician was significantly different. They generally feel more comfortable with a political project which is clear, ambitious and didactic. New Labour's project has therefore been constantly presented as being in search of itself because it has reflected our times in terms of its lack of a single central explanatory framework and because the influence of eighteen years of electoral defeat had embedded a consultative instinct. The consultative instinct could also be put down, more cynically, to an ideological insecurity.

4

It's the economy, stupid

In this section I will explore in more detail the way in which the Blair–Brown governments ended the decline debate. I will focus here on three interconnected aspects of the debate: political economy, Britain's world position and the vexed question of British identity and values. I argue that in each of these areas Margaret Thatcher proposed a strong thesis which inspired an equally strong antithesis provoking a renewal of debate. Tony Blair and Gordon Brown have produced a synthesis out of these arguments in most of these areas but there remains a strong element of discord over the racial aspects of British identity – though even here there is a confidence in British values, underpinned by a resurgence of Christian ideology, that is significantly different from the debate in previous decades. In this area they have ended the debate not by curing the problem so much as changing the argument.

The ideological uncertainty that appears to characterise the Blair–Brown consensus on the economic question is in part at least a product of affluence. Despite the views expressed by Stalin, the economic wealth of a nation has been a central feature of its vitality in the period of long European peace since 1945. In the politics of affluence that has characterised this period the extent and nature of economic performance in many ways replaced, at least within the European conversation on such issues, the role of the number of divisions of tanks and the size of missiles in determining the greatness of a nation. For social democrats the question of what to do with affluence has long been problematic.[1] Harold Macmillan summed it up in his 1959 general election campaign:

> Indeed let us be frank about it – most of our people have never had it so good. Go around the country, go to the industrial towns, go to the farms and you will see a state of prosperity such as we have never had in my lifetime – nor indeed in the history of this country.[2]

In that campaign it was the ability of the two parties to keep levels of growth high and maintain full employment while controlling inflation that dominated – Macmillan called it the '$64,000 question'. In the background there was the Cold War, the bomb and decolonialisation, but these remained in the background.

When Bill Clinton was running for the US presidency in 1992 he famously had a big sign hung in his campaign headquarters that bore the slogan 'It's the economy, stupid'. The resonance of this phrase in the political history of most democracies was recognised by the declinists and a significant part of the literature of decline was devoted to a nest of interconnected economic problems. For many of these writers the economic question was an extension of the cultural critique because Britain was a trading nation with an industrial spirit. The economic problem had five dimensions:

1. **Economic growth.** Although the UK economy grew faster in the period from 1945 than it had in the 100 years before, it grew less fast than the OECD average and less fast than the six European states that then made up the EEC. Growth become a key measure of the relative performance of a country. It did not matter that in absolute terms the British economy was

growing; what mattered was how fast it was growing in relation to other states. Britain has now caught up.

2. **Productivity in manufacturing.** The basis of the British economic miracle in the nineteenth century had been manufacturing, but its lack of competitiveness, shared with much of the rest of Europe, saw much manufacturing move to other parts of the world. Britain had a particular productivity problem, aspects of which still remain. However, so much of the rest of the economy was competitive that the failings of manufacturing mattered less economically than they did socially or even culturally.

3. **Industrial relations.** Known as the British disease, the level and frequency of strikes became a central focus of the decline debate, especially in the 1970s. This problem has virtually disappeared.

4. **Private enterprise.** From the 1950s onwards pressure groups and think tanks such as the Institute of Economic Affairs argued that Britain's tax burden and overly intrusive state undermined the ability of British entrepreneurs to generate wealth. Deregulation and structural and cultural changes are slowly solving this problem.

5. **Public ownership and public services.** From rail transport through to the NHS, a recurrent focus of the debate has been the quality and delivery of public services. In a sense this problem is insoluble because public services can never actually be good enough; however, by placing public service delivery at the top of the political agenda their future has been removed from the debate. The question is no longer whether we should have public services but rather how good those services should be.

To understand the way in which the debates on these five problems have been resolved we need to return to the defeat of the post-war Labour government. In September 1951, the

King urged Clement Attlee, the Labour Prime Minister, to resolve an uncertain political situation. Labour's massive 1945 majority had been cut at the 1950 election to five seats. At the time this margin was thought to be unsustainable. The King wanted to go on a long foreign trip and did not like leaving Britain while the question was unresolved. Attlee was happy to oblige, not least because his great enemy Herbert Morrison was out of the country. The Prime Minister called the election in a broadcast, the first time this had happened. No government has gone to the country in a worse state than Attlee's did in 1951, and no newspaper during the campaign predicted anything other than a Conservative win. Nonetheless, Labour narrowed the Tory lead during the campaign and succeeded in getting their core support out. Labour polled more votes over the country as a whole than any other party until John Major's Conservatives in 1992, but the votes did not translate into seats.

The 1951 election ended the post-war Labour governments, put Labour into opposition for thirteen years and marked the start of a decade of bitter internecine warfare in the party. But it was not an unqualified disaster. The test of the greatness of a government must surely be how long its achievements last. If defeat destroys not just the administration but also the ethos and project of the government then that test has failed. If, on the other hand, the incoming government plays out the hand it has been dealt then we can talk of a great government, a government that has shaped its age. The Attlee government lost power in 1951 but it had shaped the agenda for the decades that followed.

It had been a great government, but by the end it was a divided one. Leading ministers who were healthy enough (many, including Attlee, were in and out of hospital) spent their time fighting each other. It was an exhausted government, physically and in terms of ideas. The small majority after the 1950 election was not considered a mandate for action, which was convenient because by then Labour ministers did not really have a clue what to do next. The Conservative campaign in 1951, much like Blair's campaign in 1997, set out to reassure the country that the Attlee settlement would be safe with them. The message was competence, freedom from controls and a new direction with a new team – especially in an uncertain world with security problems related to oil in the Middle East. That call to freedom was based not on rolling back the nationalisation or the planning apparatus that Attlee had created, but on putting up a barrier to any further advance. The consensus forged by Attlee survived on questions of state ownership, on the centrality of full employment and on the role of the UK as the USA's key ally. But Attlee paid a heavy price in the election for his support of the US intervention in Korea.

Attlee had committed Britain to the war in Korea and his Chancellor, Hugh Gaitskell, was pushing through Cabinet a massive and in the event undeliverable rearmament budget to pay for it. Attlee's view was simple: this was about duty, playing one's part in the Atlantic community. But the rearmament package was crippling the government's ability to make broader promises on developing the welfare state. The sense of intellectual and policy paralysis echoes across the decades. Just after the election there was a Labour conference on policy making. Aneurin Bevan made a fascinating speech in which he argued that the Labour movement needed to look beyond these shores to the problems of the colonies and dependent territories, that in a sense the domestic problem had been solved and the agenda now was to cure the world. It was a powerful speech and it has its echoes in the Commission for Africa and the debt relief plan that Blair and Brown championed. The only caution that should be offered to the present is that Attlee's government was to a significant extent consumed by foreign and defence issues, and took its eye off the domestic ball.

Though Labour lost in 1951, they did not feel like they had lost. Hugh Dalton, the former Chancellor, noted, 'Election results very good. Casualties minimised, especially among our young. How wise we Octobrists were! . . . The election results are wonderful. We are out at just the right moment.' Richard Crossman was struck by 'the cheerfulness and morale of the party, compared with its state of semi-disintegration before the election'. Such complacency contributed to Labour's long stay in the wilderness. Labour's failure to articulate its own next phase (the election manifesto of 1951 was extremely short on new ideas), and the general drift in Labour policy making in the first half of the 1950s, allowed the result in 1951 to be the end of the collectivist stream of policy making rather than its beginning. The parallel with 1997 is clear. The road not taken in 1951 was the road away from much of the core agenda of 1945. But the consequences of the consensus-building election of 1951 were not the triumph of a progressive agenda, any more than the election of the Blair–Brown government in 1997 represented the triumph of Thatcherism. Consensus formation is not the same as moving forward. When Winston Churchill came in, his team of younger ministers were intent on freezing state ownership where it was. They did not want a developmental state; they wanted to roll it back where they could. They wanted the post-war legislation to be a settlement: thus far and no further. Alfred Sherman now calls the Conservative governments of the 1990s 'the Thatcher interlude', by which he means that even under Major the New Right agenda of reducing the role of the state was stalled. Under Labour it was frozen. It is not actually the case that Labour has pushed ahead in any very meaningful way with Thatcher's anti-statist policy formation. Rather there has been a Thatcher settlement, and Labour's policy started from there.

That it started from there might lead to the logical conclusion that it must have been Thatcher who ended the decline debate rather than Blair and Brown. But Thatcher cannot claim to have done that, because her project for reversing decline inspired a significant set of historically informed programmatic critiques. The classic statement of thinking dialectically is that there is a thesis that produces its antithesis. From the thesis and the antithesis comes the synthesis. Thatcherism was a thesis in the decline debate which produced a powerful antithesis. The interplay of these two aspects of the dialectics of our age emerged in the ideological synthesis which defined the goverment elected in 1997.

Above and beyond this process of synthesis, Thatcher had not actually reached a view on core issues that could have been sustainable over a long period unless ideologically committed and heavily polarised governments continued to be elected. For example, she did not have a sustainable response to the problem of Britain's world position. The historical lesson that mass unemployment, because of its impact on individual lives and social fabrics, was a more meaningful manifestation of decline because it had been more central to how democracies perish was lost on Thatcher. Instead for her it was trade union militancy and inflation, as we have already discussed, that mattered most. Moreover she was not interested in making people feel comfortable about being part of the new consensus; hers was a politics of the enemy within, of 'us and them' and the wet and the dry. She suggested that the pace of radical transformation needed to be maintained.

There was a universalism at the end of the Thatcherite road, a market universalism. To what extent was it the claim to universalism, inherent in the Bevanite interpretation of the

Attlee programme not as a settlement but a foundation, that caused people – the floating voters – to vote for the Tories, who promised universalism's benefits without extending its costs? To what extent was it also the claim to universalism – of a market variety – in the Thatcher settlement that equally though over a much longer period scared those voters off? What the Conservatives of the 1950s and New Labour of the 1990s promised were the fruits of a new system without the logical consequences: in the 1950s a mixed economy that offered a safety net and full employment with all the benefits of affluence; in the 1990s a free-market economy with better provision of public goods and suitable noises about the removal of the underclass.

The Blair–Brown synthesis, in a way similar to the Churchill government after 1951, was not the solution of problems so much as the ending of that phase of the debate. In the ending of this debate I would suggest that the first four out of the main problems of political economy (see above) have been cured or neutralised and that their power to influence or shape political debate has been ended. The fifth had two distinct elements, which have been torn apart. The first element, the public ownership of industry, has been resolved – the state does not own companies any longer. The second part, public service, is now top of the political agenda and is being debated mostly in terms of means and not ends: everyone now agrees that public services have to get better rather than be replaced. This level of consensus – the ending of the argument – was not possible under Thatcher because the discourse and public policy priorities of Thatcherism had been dedicated to removing the state from both the owner-ship of industry and the running of services.

Thatcherism was based on the supposed rediscovery of a nineteenth-century idea of greatness and entrepreneurial spirit but, as many critics, such as David Marquand, have pointed out, it fundamentally misunderstood or deliberately understated the role of the state and of public intervention in the creation of both the idea and the actuality of that greatness. So in terms of the reversal of decline that the Thatcherites were claiming, there was no renewal of even the greatness that they claimed to be remaking because there was no renewal or reinvention of the constructive role of the state. The greatness that might be claimed for the Thatcher project is essentially the renewal of competitiveness within the private sector and a language of profit which placed this at the forefront of business activity. In this sense, and in their own terms, Thatcherites returned to some aspects of the nineteenth century but neither brought together the combination of elements that the Victorians mastered, nor updated these to reflect the contemporary realities they faced.

In contrast, beginning under Major, but more significantly under Blair and Brown, the importance of the partnership between public institutions delivering public goods – education, health and so on – and private institutions generating profits has been recognised. As with other aspects of the argument presented in this book, I am not therefore suggesting that the economic problems of this country have been solved. I am suggesting that the problems as articulated in the body of literature that I earlier identified as comprising the decline debate have been resolved. The longest stretch of unbroken economic growth for 100 years and the beginning of the renewal of public services in partnership with private profit suggest that what used to be known as 'objective reality' would support going beyond the mere claim that an argument had been settled, but the really interesting question for the contemporary historian in all this is what the major economic problems we now face are and how they differ from those in the past.

If domestic politics has not settled into a broadly based consensus then the weight of the meaning of political difference needs to be evaluated. To make sense of this we should consider again the first post-war decades. After 1951 an economic consensus was in operation but there were extremes in both parties who articulated profound and polarised differences on substantial policy questions – the ownership of industry, the use of taxation, the boundaries of the state. They were not bickering about inessentials. It is important to try to re-enter the mindset of the time to understand the extent of the accommodation that had been achieved between two substantially different world views. Collectivism, the planned economy, ownership by the state and universal welfare were ideas and approaches which still occupied meaningful space on the political spectrum. Their opposites – privatisation, selective welfare, monetarism – were in the same position. In many elections they operated at the margins of the major parties' manifestos, not in the centre of the programmes, but they were a credible part of the conversation, and at key moments they took centre stage.

Compare that position with the nature, texture and feel of debate today. On domestic economic issues – the use of direct progressive taxation, the ownership of industry (except perhaps the railways), the role of the state, the notion of universalism, the concept of collectivism – there are no profound political differences. But more than this, the left does not exist on these issues. The electorate does not recognise alternatives to the neo-liberal/social market economy as at all meaningful. This is a profound shift in the parameters of the political spectrum and in the definitions of what is left and what is right. But it is not remotely the end of ideology. There is a vibrant left which is engaged with the politics of the world; there is also the 'lifestyle left'. We will return to consider the position of the contemporary left on foreign policy and lifestyle in a moment, but for now it is worth pausing to reflect on the meaning of this deep consensus on political economy.

Many of the debates in political economy that plagued Britain since the Second World War have been resolved by merging the two main programmatic responses to the articulation of the five main economic problems as outlined above. These problems, with education underpinning them, generated the two principal accounts of why Britain declined from being a global economic power in the post-war years.

These accounts are linked to two main proposals for what could be done to stop the process and restore greatness. As stated earlier, the first is statist. The statists worked out complex plans for reversing Britain's path to destitution. Their basic idea can be summed up as State Action. Britain fell in the post-war world because it did not have a developmental state. Putting the state back in has dominated their thinking because, though not always practitioners, they believe in politics. They believe in the ability of the state, usually a small, well-run state, to spend money well and make the right laws to create the circumstances in which Britain can be great. The Labour Party in power has, periodically, followed some of these ideas.

The second proposal comes from the individualists. Beginning with Arthur Seldon at the Institute of Economic Affairs in the 1960s, and moving through Alfred Sherman and Keith Joseph, whom we discussed earlier, and reflected in the work of John Redmond and others, this group had a simple idea for saving Britain: reduce state action. Britain was failing to compete in the modern world because of excessive state intervention and control. The people needed to be set free. Taking the state out and promoting individualism were key. Virtually ignored by Conservative governments before 1970, this set of ideas became the governing ideology that became Thatcherism. Blair and Brown have merged the two.

This takes us back to J. K. Galbraith. In *The Culture of Contentment* he divided society in the new economy into the contented, the uncertain and the underclass, with the uncertain moving between the underclass and the contented depending on the particular economic circumstances. New Labour has endorsed a consensus that is the political expression of Galbraith's thesis. Their management of the economy has so far enabled them to minimise the slippage of the uncertain into the underclass, but the gap between rich and poor has reached a forty-year high. In the new definition of who is a member of our polity, of our contented class, the phrase 'you've never had it so good' springs to mind. For the middle group, the insecure, the part-time workers in debt or at the threshold of welfare, jobs exist and low mortgage rates allow greater security from negative equity, at least for now. While once in the long-gone days of real full employment security would have been more meaningful, survival is possible and if public services improve further we might even see a closing of the gap between what Galbraith once called private affluence and public squalor. The paradox of contemporary politics is that there is little or no significant political voice calling for intervention by the state to close this gap or cure this poverty, hardly any pressure to break the marriage of the public and the private. While there are significant problems with the reality of income distribution and the spread of property ownership, while there are still pockets of long-term unemployment and relative deprivation, there is little or no significant debate about how to deal with these problems, no constituency supporting significant increases in public investment, no set of commentators demanding the state be further rolled back to allow the market to sort things out.

The consensus is so deeply rooted that it is only public service and not public employment or ownership that will alleviate the uncertainties of the middling group. There is no grand blueprint for the transformation of their lives, for embedding security or providing a universal safety net. The contemporary ambition of progressive politicians and the slowly emerging alternative from David Cameron's Conservatives is the promise to keep the uncertain from falling into the underclass. Perhaps it is this that defines both the ambition of contemporary government and the role of the state: not a safety net or the elimination of an underclass, but the minimisation of slippage from a life of uncertainty and insecurity to a life in the underclass.

There is clearly a historical break by the Conservatives when they endorse the current consensus on the role of public services, but there is also historic change for Labour. The new political consensus, forged from Thatcherism by the Blair–Brown governments, incorporated 'enterprise' into a political economy that says it will not simply accept mass unemployment as a price worth paying for profits, has ambitious targets for poverty reduction and has done much to deal with long-term youth unemployment. Nevertheless, it is a politics that is far removed from the democratic socialism of Bevan, Wilson or Foot or even the social democracy of Gaitskell, Kinnock and Smith. Indeed, it is hard to escape the feeling that a John Smith government would have retained a broader vision of who was to be included and though it too might have produced a synthesis from the polarised debates of the 1980s and 1990s, its basis would have been different. A Michael Foot government would have aimed at something close to universalism. The Blair–Brown governments have narrowed the definition of the included and endorsed and deepened the consensus that accepts a permanent underclass of the excluded.

For the radicals of the right the broad acceptance of the new consensus is a setback rather than a defeat. For the radicals of the left it represents a much longer-term reversal. My colleague Philip Spencer argues that the lack of a programmatic critique of Blair–Brown from the left is due to the contempt felt by the intellectual left opposition for the social democratic left and a sense that New Labour does not merit a new critique. This presupposes that when this left opposition did articulate a critique it was in some sense meaningful. It assumes that the New Left/Trotskyite critique of capitalism that was put forward in the 1970s and rose to a high tide in the Alternative Economic Strategy (which argued for a siege economy and widespread nationalisation) was plausible, that there was a moment at which transformatory politics was one possible outcome of the breakdown of the Attlee settlement. I do not believe that this moment ever actually existed. But whether or not it existed in terms of what was achievable in policy terms, it certainly existed in the content of the debate and in the positions taken by commentators, historians and others. All such voices have since been quietened to the point of oblivion – the contemporary silence of the left on matters of political economy is deafening.

Many have welcomed the contemporary policy settlement but overall, though it represents a compromise, it should primarily be seen as a defeat for the left and it is in the size and permanence of the underclass that the meaning of the new consensus can best be understood and the extent of the left's defeat in the ending of the decline debate seen. The acceptance of such an underclass by the left would have been unthinkable forty years ago. Now, once through welfare-to-work and out the other side, it is largely ignored. It does not form the basis for the rallying cries of a generation of radical analysts of Britain's relative position. The fates of sink estates and single parents do not attract the left intellectuals to their cause. The great heroes of the left today, in an uncanny echo of the last period of consensus in the 1950s, speak of the world's problems more readily and more often than they do of our own. Aneurin Bevan's great critique, *In Place of Fear*, claimed that many of the big domestic questions had been solved. Building on the themes of his 1951 speech mentioned earlier, it argued that it was a time for democratic socialists to broaden their horizons and consider the state of the world, particularly the need for colonial development. The energy and drive in that book are on issues of decolonisation, development and foreign policy. The obsessions of the contemporary left are equally focused abroad rather than at home.

The outward-looking nature of the contemporary left is accounted for quite simply. As in the 1950s they offer no meaningful alternative to the consensual political economy they face. The difference is that they created the consensus of the 1950s and have either endorsed that of the 1980s and 1990s or been left emasculated by it. The similarities between the two periods are striking. It was the Conservative Party that benefited most from the consensus of the late 1940s. In 1951, 1955 and 1959 the Conservative Party said, 'We will not touch the basic gains you have made as individuals from the Attlee settlement but we will run the rest of the economy and everything else better than they did. Also, we will not extend universalism further than it has already gone.' In the 1990s the roles were reversed. Labour could basically argue that they would now run the market consensus. They would not reverse any of the reforms of Thatcherism but would run public services better. In other words, they would allow floating voters to feel better about being neo-liberal individualists because of a language of compassion towards the underclass. Ironically therefore, in both cases it was the political parties that had been forced to compromise with the consensus through electoral pressure who became trusted with its operation – even in 1964 the Tories nearly pulled off another victory. In the 1950s there was to the right of the mainstream Conservative Party a well-argued alternative to the politics of the consensus, which gradually, as the decade progressed, came in from the cold. It is hard to find any recognisable alternative project on British domestic political economy today. Arguing against performance-related pay for academics, against foundation hospitals and for the renationalisation of the railways does not constitute a meaningful alternative domestic programme.

It could be that the political and cultural space for such radical alternatives is closed off. People with a radical self-image express it in our culture through their sense of cosmopolitan concerns, and in the anti-globalisation and anti-war movements. Or it could be that the constituency for a radical domestic alternative simply does not exist. Again there are parallels with the 1950s but the analogy is not perfect. Left intellectuals in the 1950s were concerned with decolonisation and the bomb but they also had a significantly different political economy to offer in the form of nationalisation and the state running of the economy.

This other left has turned in on itself. Beginning in the 1930s in the writings of Aldous Huxley and others, the notion of internal escape from arguments about the world that could not be won was born. Politics as self-realisation amounts to an abdication of moral and political responsibility for the world around you. The left turned to self-help, lifestyle, the pursuit of the private, when it had lost the battle for control of the public. Ironically it was the market reforms of the 1980s that allowed lifestyle choice to be merged with marketing to produce a form of what appeared to be an alternative economy but was in fact a high-end consumer service sector for massage, aromatherapy and green lifestyles.

That the left critique on domestic policy has been vanquished should offer little comfort to those on the right who supported the idea that Margaret Thatcher was Hayek's Lenin. The grand critique of the right has been implemented through privatisation, labour market liberalisation and lower taxes – very little of the Thatcher settlement has been reversed. But this is not meant to imply that the right have won on all counts. The Thatcher agenda was pushed to the point, as I have argued, of far-reaching reform rather than revolution. Both sides have given ground, both extremes have left the field and the discourse and the policy making have settled down in the centre. That the right finds it difficult to mount a sustained attack or connect that attack to the course of British history is hardly surprising; they set the course. The strongest parallels in terms of general elections are between the meaning of 1951 and the meaning of 1997.

This absence on the left of a meaningful critique of Tony Blair's project also raises the question of why he came to be hated by so much of the liberal establishment. After all, at first glance, he is one of them in a way that Gordon Brown is not. They spent eighteen years praying for deliverance but they hated the deliverer very quickly – at least this is the picture which the commentary pages of the liberal newspapers most often present as being the case. In fact the dimensions of Blair's standing are more complex than this. He was never actually one of the liberal elite as he appeared on the surface to be. His faith, an issue I will return to later, made him different from the mainstream of London liberal life. He was also different because his project was always actually much more mainstream and nationalistic than was their world view. But the complexity of Blair is also reflected in the complexity of what we mean by the left-liberal establishment in post-decline Britain. This question is most obviously complex and difficult to answer when we consider Britain's role in the world.

5

Britain and the world

Back in the twentieth century, when Stalin was asking his question about the Pope, power was still about guns and butter – the guns seemed to have the edge. The question of firepower, size and strength dominated. These things still count even though the nature of the enemy has changed. In the age of Al Qaeda the small terrorist group can represent as significant a security challenge for a state as Stalin's divisions once did. However, foreign policy remains concerned with other states and their relation to ourselves. As Andrew Gamble and David Reynolds have both argued, global status is about perception and relations. Even more than the economic indicators, debate in this area must be about relative rather than absolute decline.

There are four kinds of issue:

1. the loss of empire
2. the relationship between the UK and the EU
3. the special relationship with the USA
4. the national question in the UK.

Broadly two positions emerged from these problems – a 'world-power position', which argued for the replacement of imperial greatness by acting as the Greeks to the Americans' Romans, maintaining the unity of the UK and a distance from the European Union, and a 'European-power position', which accepted devolution within the UK and an ever-closer relationship with the other members of the EU. Though there are clear policy choices to be made here, the options are between ways in which Britain can punch above its weight – a European way or an Atlantic way. Isolationism or neutralism are not part of the debate.

The loss of the British Empire was part of a process of modernisation and not of decline. The notion that the loss of empire signifies decline because of some absolute measure of power in terms of land area ruled is patently absurd in a nuclear age. Britain enjoyed more power in the nuclear age than before because its position was based on the current and future technology rather than on the technology and strategic choices of the past. But more importantly, surrendering empire, sometimes under pressure and defeat and sometimes voluntarily because of a judgement on the balance of self-interest between retreat and clinging to the wreckage, was a process of maturing as a democracy. Power and status were vested in the well-being of the British people rather than in the oppression of other people. This provided much greater domestic stability as the balance of world power shifted and the empire became unsustainable; moreover, being on the winning side in two world wars helped to prevent the regime change and the political instability suffered by other major colonial powers. The speed of withdrawal from empire, the incorporation of the Labour movement into government from the 1920s onwards and the creation of the welfare state after 1945 are also significant factors in making the end of empire a sign of progress and not regression.

Nevertheless the feeling that it is somehow important that Britain should count for something in the world is a very real one. The parameters of the debate were set by Winston Churchill's three circles: Europe, the Commonwealth and the United States. In a sense the decline debate was about how best to maintain this balancing act, linking the circles and avoiding disappearing into the centre of one of them. The post-war settlement crafted by Ernest Bevin was to place Britain firmly at the junction of the north Atlantic and the Commonwealth circles, with a greater distance from Europe. After Suez, this settlement was effectively shattered and the orientation of Britain, like some immense oil tanker, was shifted towards Europe. It took decades of debate, but eventually even the Labour Party accepted our European future.

In political economy there is a sense in which New Labour has attempted to fuse arguments from outside the Labour tradition (neo-liberalism) with elements that it is more familiar with, for example public service. In terms of Britain's world role the unfolding of the debate and its resolution into something which has strong elements of consensus but still falls short of the level of agreement achieved on domestic policy is much more rooted in internal Labour disputes and history. As the party developed its thinking on Britain's place in the world during the post-war period, the key arguments evolved in a series of phases. In the first the disagreement was about how best to achieve a leading position in a bipolar world: should Britain support the USA or take a third-way or third-force position, prompting an image of Britain sitting at the global head table; the conflict was about the form of leadership that would achieve that place: political or moral. Bevin settled this argument early on with the creation of NATO and the push for political leadership.

The second phase was characterised by the gradual readjustment, the extremely slow readjustment, to Britain's reduced status. Conflict centred on how best to respond, after Suez, to the simultaneous pressures of EEC, decolonisation and US economic power. This phase was the longest and most complex for the Labour Party. It was only resolved after years of schism and four electoral defeats by the adoption of European social democracy and the ending of the Cold War. The third phase was the post-Cold War phase, in which the issue of domestic unilateralism was removed and the question became centred on the role of the EU in maintaining Britain's global position.

New Labour's foreign and defence policy can therefore be understood as the culmination of a series of significant disagreements and a fusion of the moral and political strands of Labour's perception of Britain's leading role in the world. From the moral leadership strand came the commitment from Gordon Brown to tackle Third World debt, increase spending on aid and use the EU as an instrument of poverty reduction as much as wealth creation. From the political leadership strand came the Atlanticist and interventionist policy of Tony Blair and Jack Straw in a succession of cases: Kosovo, Afghanistan and Iraq. Disarmament as a form of moral leadership and unilateral intervention as a form of political leadership have disappeared. Liberal interventionism underpinned by patriotism and the centrality of Britain's right and potential as a world leader are at the forefront. David Miliband's new diplomacy will continue this trend, albeit with greater multilateralism.

Margaret Thatcher's anti-European instincts ensured that the debate on Britain's world position remained central. The Falklands War created the aura of a return to greatness and counting for something. But it is the special relationship with the United States that continued to have the greatest impact on Britain's ability to punch above her weight on the world stage. We are now in the curious position of having a pro-European government that is committed to the future of the EU but which continues to place as great a value on the special relationship with the USA and has endorsed the sense of irrelevance of the Commonwealth in British strategy. It is a complex situation but notice that whichever way the weight of Britain's future global position falls it will ensure that the UK remains a significant player on the world scene. There is no isolationist position. If the EU develops a common foreign and defence policy then Britain could choose to be at the forefront of a major new alliance or remain as the defender of NATO among the 'new European' nations. If it does not, then Britain can continue to assert influence through the special relationship with the USA. In either case there is no sense of British decline or irrelevance.

The paradox is that much of the country seems comfortable with this approach to the world and supportive of the need to fight the global war on terrorism aggressively both in terms of the direct anti-terrorist legislation and in the wider sense of a cultural war of identity in which asylum seekers and immigrants are represented as security threats. The majorities that supported the invasion of Iraq did so because they had been persuaded of the potential threat; while this could have been seen as the irrational response of a gullible population to the use of fear by cynical politicians, the London bombings made the threat seem tangible. The swing against the war was based on the revelations of lying, the misuse of intelligence and, perhaps more importantly, the failure to uncover the WMD that could be used against British targets. The detail, that the WMD that were supposed to be there could not have reached the UK, does not diminish the extent to which people have felt threatened. Blair articulated the nature of the fear that exists rather than creating it.

For the liberal establishment this fear is irrational and the means by which Blair set out to combat it unnecessarily draconian. Therefore the issue of the war in Iraq became a touchstone for many of the failings of the government and the flaws in Blair's personality in terms of Britain's position in the world. Moreover, it is the Arab world that should be in fear of the UK rather than the other way around. The liberal establishment's newspapers presented President Bush and Prime Minister Blair as the 'terrorists', the peace wreckers and the 'real threat' to world peace. These fears were fed in 2002 when Robert Cooper, a foreign policy adviser to Blair, argued for a new imperialism. In a pamphlet published by the Foreign Policy Centre, he stated:

> When dealing with the more old-fashioned kinds of states outside the postmodern continent of Europe, we need to revert to the rougher methods of an earlier era – force, pre-emptive attack, deception . . . The opportunities, perhaps even the need, for colonisation is [*sic*] as great as it ever was in the 19th century . . . What is needed, then, is a new kind of imperialism . . . We can already discern its outline: an imperialism which, like all imperialism, aims to bring order and organisation but which rests today on the voluntary principle.[1]

This was the mistake of hubris that Thatcher made in her worst moments. The temptation to read Britain's involvement in an all-too-brief era of humanitarian intervention as a translation of Britain's past to current policy or a mere capitulation to the influence of the neo-conservatives in the USA is misplaced. The defenders of Blair's wars argue that they were not fought with imperialist objectives in mind and that the neo-cons are not imperialists. There has been in almost everything written about neo-cons in the UK a fundamental misunderstanding. They are not imperialist or colonialist in the traditional sense of the words, not even capitalist imperialists in the traditional American sense of the word. There is a deep strain of long-term isolationism in their thinking that is usually ignored. In a way there is a failure to grasp the depth and ambition of the project upon which they are embarked. British hawks argue that the left liberal press, political class and intelligentsia have fundamentally failed to take the right seriously enough.

Supporters of the neo-con position in the UK, such as the Henry Jackson Society, suggest that the long-term ambition of American neo-conservatives is to make the world safe for Americans. This would entail, if it were adopted by the US government, no more short-term fixes with dictators but investing in the long-term predictability of democracy. In relations between states there has been a paradigm shift, but it takes us a long time to see that shift in politics, just as it does in the sciences. It takes us a long time to see that the old world has gone and the new is taking shape. The people we call neo-cons, the Jacksonians suggest, saw the shift first and saw it clearest; there is now a fundamental failure to acknowledge that it is the future that the USA offers to the UK and not the past. We trade in goods and services with Europe but our strategic future lies with North America – as it has done since 1945. If we are to protect the weak and vulnerable and if we are to spread the ideas of democracy around the world to make our own future safer then dictatorships cannot be trusted and therefore must be destroyed.

So either Britain is the major threat to world peace because it is a terrorist state or Britain in alliance with the USA is set on a project to make the world safe for democracy. In neither case is Britain the weak, enfeebled 'sick man of Europe', incapable of defining a role for itself in the world, mesmerised by debates on the regulation of its sausage industry by the EU or incapacitated by a policy-making elite too timid to grasp the reality of the world. The contemporary debate about Britain's world position is not one shaped by the self-image of a nation in decline. It is shaped by the self-image of a nation in the ascendant – the question is, which summit should contemporary Britain seek to climb? The winner in that argument may well be the one who can integrate a sustainable sense of

British identity into the structure of their policy approach. We have come back over and over again in this book to the question of culture, to the question that underpinned the angst-ridden texts of the great decline debate – who are we?

Whose decline, whose country?

In considering the case for New Labour having reversed British decline we have looked so far at what can be called conventional areas of political discussion and debate. Another set of problems that the decline literature has engaged with concerns the way in which the identity of the British people is constructed, described and experienced. Questions of identity can never be entirely solved. No national culture can ever be entirely 'at ease with itself'; indeed, it is difficult to know what such a phrase is supposed to mean. However, there can be periods of more or less intense dispute about the meaning of an identity and there can be periods in which this debate threatens the unity of the nation state itself.

The very phrase 'identity of the British people' invites another book because it opens up so many different dimensions. Who are the British? Which nation or nations are they part of? Which nations should make up Britain? How many identities can an individual British person have at any one time? How has the nature of identity changed and how will it change further? Can you have multiple identities if the values that are at the heart of these identities are contested? Is a more complex or layered identity in some sense a less strong or real one? What does it mean to talk about a decline or an erosion of the British identity?

The multinational nature of the British state and the extended community of British expatriates around the world have always made the question of a British identity problematic.

The place you were born forms the first kind of identity question. To speak of an English identity or a Scottish or a Welsh one makes more sense. This in turn is made more complex in the era of immigration. Then the development of new social movements from the 1960s added the aspects of gender and sexual identity to the question. Back in the 1930s the *Encyclopedia of the Social Sciences* (New York: Macmillan, 1930–5) did not have an entry on identity, 'but it does have one on identification – largely focused on finger-printing'.[2] In the 1980s and 1990s the literature on identity became all-pervasive.

There were therefore three dimensions to the identity part of the great decline debate:

1. the national question
2. the lifestyle question
3. the race question.

The national question

For Margaret Thatcher to have ended the debate about British decline she would have had to resolve these three questions. But here again, as in political economy, her policies represented a thesis which, rather than producing synthesis, produced antitheses of unequal strength and intensity. Her absolute opposition to devolution for Scotland and Wales and her narrow articulation of what amounted to English nationalism produced resurgence in nationalist movements in Wales and Scotland and a failure to bring peace in Northern Ireland. The overt playing of the race card on immigration and the slowness of the modernisation of British policing produced the riots in Brixton and elsewhere. The emphasis on family values and rolling back the permissive agenda produced the GLC agenda of identity politics. At the end of the 1980s and for much of the 1990s, the identity aspect of the decline debate was as intense as it had been at any point since the 1950s. The election of the Blair government did much to synthesise the positions on these debates and to suggest that in this sphere, as in political economy and world position, we are now in a new era. Devolution has taken place and, despite the recent narrow victory for the SNP, a majority of even the Scots remain comfortable with a multi-nation identity. Beyond the national question, our racial identity seems much less settled; indeed, the British model of multi-culturalism has collapsed and in its place is an uneasy coexistence between Powellite rhetoric and integrationist policy making. Though the old debates have fallen away in this area above all others, the seriousness and intensity of the new debates is perhaps even more troubling than what we saw before. Finally, the lifestyle politics of the old GLC have now been mainstreamed, but so too have family and behaviour values derived from some sections of the Christian churches that have become much more strongly political.

It was once easy to be dismissive of these kinds of question, and to an extent the concrete forms that problems of identity might take are constructed out of the problems we have already discussed: our position in the world as a country and the state of our economy. For the traditional articulation of the identity debate, this later concern was central. Over much of the post-war period the problem of identity has been tied up closely with the national structure of the United Kingdom. The identity debate has come to the fore when the distribution of wealth between different groups in the state has appeared to become structurally unsustainable. In the late 1960s we began to see some regions suffer from economic downturn more than others and this became articulated as a problem of identity. This is most obvious in the debate about the mutual relationship of the nations of the UK and, within England, the affluence of the south-east as against the relative poverty of the north: the one-nation question. This identity debate was actually deepened and broadened by the Thatcher governments. The political divisions between Scotland and England and between Northern Ireland and England were polarised.

In the quotation that begins this book, Gordon Brown cites Tom Nairn's thesis that we faced the break-up of Britain. The likelihood of this break-up has been reduced for now by devolution but it remains a distinct possibility at some future point. The major difference is that in the context of a global economy and an integrated Europe, it no longer seems unthinkable. I would go so far as to suggest that for many thirty- and fortysomething Britons, not to mention younger ones, the exact status of Scotland (even for most Scots) in the UK is irrelevant, compared to other political issues such as education and health.

In contrast the issues of lifestyle choice and sexual identity are central to the way that people express themselves. In the run-up to the 1997 election it appeared that Tony Blair was going to present a strong thesis of his own on these issues and that the ideology that was going to gain most from the 1997 election was Christianity. In the event, here again, Blair–Brown have produced a synthesis which has altered the terms of the political argument.

The lifestyle question

If you separate individual faith from the public role of the churches then Christianity becomes a political ideology competing with other ideologies to influence policy; as a cultural construction it has been prominent in political debate since 9/11. As such it has been well placed to achieve a historic breakthrough. Some called before the 1997 election for a Christian Democratic Party to run on a values programme against the major parties. The debate on whether to back your beliefs within existing political parties or to try and establish a new movement is sharply contested among Christian groups, but notice: the question was how, not whether, they should be involved in politics. More and more Christians realised that the state of contemporary politics offered them considerable scope for reversing the secular tide and shaping the values agenda of government. Many of the politically conservative among them looked longingly to the influence of the Christian right on politics in the USA, not just in terms of Bush and the Republicans in Congress but more generally in defining what constitutes dominant political issues throughout mainstream American debate. What was striking about the Blair premiership is not so much the extent to which faith-based politics influenced it but rather the extent to which faith-based policies ran alongside tolerance of different identities, fulfilment of many of the policies advocated by the GLC lifestyle agenda of the 1980s and even moves towards greater social liberalisation.

The range of Christian ginger groups in the UK is wide and increasing. The rejuvenated Christian Socialist Movement competes with the Conservative Christian Fellowship (CCF) and the Conservative Family Campaign; outside the older parties, but supported by people from both, is the Movement for Christian Democracy (MCD). The various and varying evangelical groups have all been working hard at influencing the New Labour governments. Some of these organisations pursue their causes within existing parties, while others worked hard over the course of the election cycle to influence people on specific issues, most notably abortion. They have certainly had a warm reception in No. 10 and they have developed their political agenda and campaigning techniques.

The MCD runs a morality database from which people can check the voting records of politicians, while members of the CCF have visited the USA to learn from the Christian Coalition; they, like some of the evangelical groups, are well financed and combine their Christian values teaching with neo-liberal economic positions. All the groups have gained ground considerably over the last ten years, and values politics is now much more central to political discourse.

For much of the history of the Labour Party there was an overt morality that underpinned the policy debate. This morality was frequently derived from a Christian socialist ethic, as with Stafford Cripps, but it was also often secular in nature. For example Hugh Gaitskell expressed a strong sense of the morality of his political belief while retaining agnosticism in religion. Besides the Christian socialists and the secular moralists, a third group derived a different ethical basis for their political beliefs from Marxism. Aneurin Bevan for example was clear that democratic socialism mattered because of its connection with, though not subservience to, the Marxist idea of the class struggle, and in turn this insight gave British socialism a unique moral force because it alone married the struggle to democracy. These diverse strains in British socialism were each usefully applied as the underpinning to policy and ideology as and when they were needed.

Gradually over the post-war period the basis and the consistency of these different belief systems have been attacked or undermined. Gaitskell's secular morality was clearly linked to an open and permissive view of society and social change. The reforming agenda carried through by his political heir, Roy Jenkins, while Home Secretary attempted to give liberal substance to the notion of an equal society. This liberal notion of individual freedom, a perception shared by Michael Foot and others on the Bevanite wing of the party, dominated the social and cultural agenda of the Labour government in the 1960s and 1970s. Paradoxically, the libertarian right in power launched a backlash against many of these ideas. The central notion of the Thatcherite critique, that welfare bred both dependency and economic failure, when married to the traditional social conservatism of the paternalists in the Tory Party, created a powerful imperative against the liberal agenda of the 1960s and 1970s. This forceful attempt to redefine political morality into the single notion of a Christian family and an entrepreneurial state influenced the social and cultural policy of the Thatcher years. The response of the secular left was strangely muted, in part because the other pillar of the left ideology, a connection with Marxism, came under severe attack in these years. The fall of the regimes in eastern Europe sapped much of the remaining intellectual confidence of many on the left.

This combination of an assertive Conservative morality and a collapse in the underpinning of the collectivist world view provided a unique opportunity for Christianity as an organising political idea. By basing an opposition to Thatcherism on a socially conservative creed such as Christianity, which was both internally consistent and universalist in instinct, many on the left found a response to the crisis of the end of collectivism. The victim was the relaxed liberalism of the secular reformers who had inspired a generation of political activists to campaign on sexual and lifestyle issues that had not previously formed part of the political agenda. The result is an uncomfortable mix of social and political liberalism in terms of the private lives of members of Parliament, but an overt sense of the end of a permissive or liberal approach to lifestyle politics, what the *Guardian* journalist David Walker has called New Labour's moral agenda. It was described by Iain Macwhirter in the *Scotsman* not long after Blair came to power:

But Blair's is not the crusty, kill-joy, old-school morality, of course. It is a new user-friendly Moral Majority for the Millennium, which takes a liberal view of sexual orientation and accepts things such as animal rights as moral absolutes. But it isn't all saving whales and sending messages to Gay Pride marches. There is an austere side to the Blair moral agenda. The rights we enjoy should reflect the duties we owe, as the new Clause Four puts it. In other words, you don't merely accept the right of unemployed people to receive benefit, you ask for something from them in exchange. Similarly, single mothers cannot expect to live off the state. Or rather they can, but they should be counselled that theirs is not a morally sanctioned lifestyle and encouraged back to work. For Blair, the family is the basic building block of society, and his government is increasingly going to turn towards restoring it as an institution. The current wave of rather politically correct moral activity – like the banning of tobacco advertising (Blair approves) and the debate on fox hunting (Blair personally opposed it even if the government doesn't back the Bill to abolish it) – is a preamble to moving on to the more moral orthodox terrain of moral hygiene. We already know about New Labour's attitude to welfare – that dependency has led to a generation of young people who are morally adrift because they live in a culture of worklessness. Both Frank Field and Gordon 'there-is-no-fifth-option' Brown see welfare reform as a moral imperative, as well as an economic one. Frank Field in particular has attacked the existing system for encouraging indolence and dishonesty. Like Blair, Brown and Field are communitarians, who believe that the materialism of both the right and the left has brought society to the brink of break-down. Communitarians such as the American sociologist Amitai Etzioni attack both socialists and free-marketeers for concentrating exclusively on economic growth and ignoring the quality of the society. Both Margaret Thatcher and Neil

Kinnock were libertarians – though they would have baulked at the description – in the sense that they had no political interest in preaching to people about how they should live their lives. Their politics was defined by the legacy of the Cold War, when capitalism and communism competed against each other in terms of how fast they could improve the living standards of the people. Moral discourse was squeezed out as politics became preoccupied with GNP and the number of washing machines per head. As we know, capitalism won. But curiously, things have moved on. People may be more materially prosperous, at least on the surface, but they are getting worried now about social breakdown, crime, insecurity, alienation and all the other nasties that religion used to deal with in less secular times. But the priests and ministers have been replaced by the media and politicians. I suspect that much of Blair's success is partly down to his conspicuous religious conviction. In a time when people believe most figures in public life to be corrupt and debauched, people are genuinely impressed by someone who seems to have real 'belief', and acts upon it. So prepare for campaigns against noisy neighbours, parents who don't send their children to school, children who don't do their homework. New Labour intends to re-moralise Britain. As in countries like Singapore – a country that the New Labour leader rather admires – we are going to be expected to behave in a better way.[3]

It is striking how much of Macwhirter's prediction came true – even though Frank Field did not survive in office long enough to deliver his reforms.

In this confused and confusing situation, in the context of a rapidly changing society that frequently seems to have been developing on a different moral and ethical planet to that inhabited by political thinkers, the opportunity for politically active Christians has been marked. In a moral and political vacuum any apparently coherent set of ideas will make a significant impression. As there is so little difference between the main parties on the basis of political economy, so the focus of the debate has switched to values and Christian ideology has an extensive vocabulary for talking about the politics of values. Indeed, though there are many competing value systems and value vocabularies – feminist, ecological, as well as those of other religious movements – our default position is to talk of these things in ways defined by our Christian heritage: that gives political Christians a great advantage. Moreover, neither neo-liberalism nor social democracy offers much of a basis for the values battle as it has come to be waged in contemporary Britain.

The Labour MP Stephen Timms summed up what he felt Christianity offered the party in a speech in 2002:

> Faith provided three vital contributions to the success of New Labour, contributions vital to its initial electoral success, and to its subsequent success in government too:
>
> - Christian faith provided leadership, as a remarkably large proportion of the government's leaders professed an active Christian faith;
> - it provided a new language, like the Prime Minister's talk of servants and ambassadors, which allowed new policies to be communicated successfully, without awakening memories of past political disputes and mistakes;
> - it provided vitally important new linkages to groups and communities whose support proved to be critically important.[4]

Despite these useful tools, social democracy's emphasis on equality does not sit neatly with the privileging of one set of lifestyle choices over another; the libertarian tradition within neo-liberalism has frequently been in conflict with the Conservative Party's traditional and avowedly Christian social authoritarianism. The answer appears to be a kind of triangulation in which politicians from the left and right move away from the traditional basis for their beliefs to compete within a new moral space. By accident of history and the religious beliefs of the main party leaders, this debate is then defined in terms of Christian values. It is at this point that Christianity becomes a political ideology like any other, pushing positions on policies from a range of perspectives but united by a set of core beliefs. However, state action against poverty has traditionally meant that the more liberal elements in the church did not unite with the evangelical elements influenced by the American Christian Coalition; though they had anti-abortion and pro-family beliefs in common, their economic visions were different. Christ shares Marx's fate in having his teaching used to support widely conflicting positions, and this ensures a conflict within the terms of the morality arguments between liberal and conservative Christians.

Much of the behaviour-based agenda of the Blair governments, ASBOs and the rest, has been underpinned by faith-based lessons. Christianity has an underlying body of belief and a series of defining issues on which people can be judged. Though the argument for a realignment of British politics through a new Christian Party might not be convincing, it might also not be necessary if the moral agenda is transformed by activist Christianity within the existing structures. There have been some moves in the USA by the conservative Christian Coalition to try and unite with Christians in the Democratic Party on certain core issues. This chimes with the kinds of faith-based politics we are now seeing in the UK.

As you walk out of many American churches you can collect a voter guide from the Christian Coalition. It provides information on the voting record and position of any candidates running in your local elections. It will especially focus on the candidate's record on abortion and condemn that candidate, irrespective of party, if they are pro-choice. Abortion and stem cell research are now the crucial issues, especially abortion: being pro-life is the litmus test of any candidate for a militant conservative. It is now more divisive an issue than either class or race. Up until now this has kept the Christian Coalition very much in the Republican camp, both because more pro-lifers were there and because the coalition also adopted a series of right-wing economic positions and, paradoxically, defended gun ownership. Though in Britain the spread and nature of the churches and of Christians are different – the Catholic Church is further to the left and the Church of England still resistant to evangelical or political pressure – the politicisation of the church is also happening. Organised groups with core values, anti-abortion, anti-gay and pro-family, have become increasingly important over the course of the New Labour government.

Blair signalled the move early on in his government. Even while still in opposition, he gave an interview to the *Telegraph*,[5] the headline of which claimed he had said that it was impossible to be a Christian and a Conservative. The movement gathered pace with the Jubilee 2000 campaign. Will Hutton reported the upsurge in Christian activism around the campaign in 1999:

> I doubt many readers know the Old Testament books of Leviticus, Exodus and Deuteronomy any more than I do, but . . . at the end of an increasingly secular century, it has been the biblical proof and moral imagination of religion that have torched the principles of the hitherto unassailable citadels of international finance – and opened the way to a radicalism about capitalism whose ramifications are not yet fully

understood . . . The left of centre should take note; it is no longer Morris, Keynes and Beveridge who inspire and change the world – it's Leviticus.[6]

Five years later, Tom Baldwin reported:

But the forces being unleashed by the furore are, for me, more troubling than the proposal itself. Concepts of vice and virtue are creeping back into our heroically secular British political culture. The moral agenda against gambling also finds an echo in other current debates on smacking children, gay civil partnerships, smoking in public, 24-hour drinking and anti-social behaviour. And, yes, the next one up will be abortion.[7]

And at the end of 2006, Joan Bakewell, writing in the *Independent*, indicated that Christian activism had not gone away:

Indeed Christian churches are increasingly active in this country's political decisions. Earlier this year, the churches led the campaign against the Assisted Dying Bill, which was defeated in the House of Lords by forty-eight votes. There are some twenty-seven bishops sitting there, roused to vote in unison by the public declarations of their leader, the Archbishop of Canterbury. But the Catholic Cardinal Archbishop of Westminster had also been effective, encouraging the many local groups to protest in what an official of Dignity in Dying called 'the biggest political campaign in church history'.

There was an even more effective campaign this autumn, when the government's proposal to impose quotas on faith schools was first mooted. The Catholic Church went into overdrive. Priests were instructed to alert their congregations, who in turn were asked to contact their MPs. The flood of letters did the job, the proposal was dropped almost immediately, and the Church, as the Cardinal Archbishop himself told me, was delighted to have been so effective.

Cardinal Murphy-O'Connor had of course been to Edinburgh to support the Make Poverty History lobby. It remains to be seen whether he will now join his fellow archbishop Rowan Williams in his opposition to the renewal of the nuclear sub Trident. Will priests and congregations be mobbing MPs over that?

. . . The churches, by now familiar with how to sway policy, have been at it again, vigorously opposing the legislation. The Catholic Archbishop of Birmingham actually had the gall to claim that the government was imposing its own moral agenda on the church. Religions in this country are free in law to preach that homosexuality is an abomination, but they are not entitled to impose such views on the rest of us. Currently this law is on hold, while Ruth Kelly, the Cabinet's devout Catholic, and Blair, possibly its soon-to-be convert, bend to religious pressure.[8]

If the voting system changes to proportional representation and the traditional coalitions of Labour and Conservative break up, then the role of small religious parties will be enhanced and the power of pressure groups on single issues such as abortion will be magnified. At the very least Christians will continue to set the terms of the values debate in a political scene dominated by questions of personal and collective moralities; in a country facing a crisis in family life and suffering the social consequences of sustained poverty in urban centres, their influence on policy could well be profound.

The scope for Christianity to influence actual policy may depend on the extent to which conventional secular devices for dealing with moral or ethical questions in politics are allowed to function. Throughout the New Labour era there have been conferences and commissions on the question of governance and standards in public life. One of the early ones, the Committee for Standards in Public Life, was first chaired by Lord Nolan. The Nolan committee's exploration of standards failed to register any discernible response in the media or among voters. 'Nolan' is now a permanent feature of public life and the speed with which his reports pass into obscurity is an indication that focusing on governance may not be the best way of breathing new life into the body politic. Rather than attempting to improve our feeling about politics, the real challenge is to maintain the existing level of public belief and engagement. In this respect an overtly Christian political appeal may be irrelevant against an unstoppable rejection of conventional politics.

Instead of evangelical politics, the Major governments attempted to shift the emphasis onto a consideration of governance. Improving governance replaced deregulation, which in turn replaced planning, as the mantra of the governing class for curing the crisis in politics. Some want to reform in order to preserve the essence of the existing system of what Peter Hennessy calls 'government by good chaps', others want to revolutionise so that their people become the good chaps. The folks, to use *Primary Colors* parlance, are evoked as being for whom the times change, but the folks stubbornly refuse to give a damn about 90 per cent of these debates. They understood planning because it made a material difference to their lives. They reacted to deregulation because it might have made a difference to the services they received, but governance – who sits on what board, what community the local spending bodies thinks it is connected to, even the electoral system or the existence of the House of Lords – these things mean nothing to most people. The active citizen, in these terms, is largely a myth invented by those employed in the middle-class welfare, educational and constitutional state apparatus to justify their own existence – Nolan and his recommendations are in part an affirmation of these people's working lives and in part a kind of professional narcissism.

Rather than being at the low point of apathy from which things can only get better, we might well be on the threshold of an entirely new scale of disillusionment and even of democratic failure – the old declining Britain was, paradoxically, characterised by high levels of political participation. In this situation good governance is no more than a convenient alibi for the failure of the political classes to deal effectively with moral issues. When politicians continue to be faced by indifference, alienation and more and more hostility, they can say, 'But we tried to put our house in order.' Nolan's response when challenged on this point is revealing. Asked why he had not recommended a system of full financial disclosure on the American model, to try and produce a real 'felt' change, he replied that this would necessarily reduce the quality and experience of members of Parliament. But if the quality and experience of members of Parliament is so high, then why does his committee exist? It exists so that politicians can feel better about themselves and do not have to face the uncomfortable truth that they are irredeemably compromised in the eyes of the people. It exists so that other public sector professionals can feel connected to a body politic with a history in which public service was rewarded and valued. They want to feel like public servants, they want to be Victorian nation builders and civic heroes. This is the central paradox of the Nolan committee. Rather than being a mechanism for creating a new kind of civic culture for voters, it is a form of psychotherapy for the middle classes who run the ever-expanding British state and quasi-state.

The committee's purpose is to give meaning to those who make what David Marquand evocatively terms the public domain – a land between private relations and the market – work. It might be that a historically unusual period, created partly by the experience of total war and partly by Keynesianism, in which a small majority of the folks believed in the efficacy of politics and had a kind of passive trust – relative, conditional, largely secular and far from universal – in their elected representatives, has ended. We have returned to the normality of a politics in which the majority of the folks feel mistrust, alienation and apathy towards their representatives and party allegiance does not feature in the way they construct their identities. In this situation we need to scale down our expectations of civic society, accepting that it will be relatively impoverished and concentrate our energy – and this is another challenge that the positivist language of politics too often brushes over – in defending existing levels of participation, accountability and citizenry. If we are at the beginning of a deeper decline in people's connection with politics then we need to set about trying to maintain the public domain which survives. This might mean accepting the inevitability of the passive and apathetic citizen; ridding ourselves of notions of a civic culture based on Victorian levels of population and ways of making laws; building a new civic culture, recognising that universal suffrage has reduced levels of participation and contemporary political practice has resulted in deep and permanent cynicism about politics.

We would be accepting failure. The new civic culture would be inclusive but would acknowledge that most of the folks will never take part and simply do not care. Public intellectuals, politicians, think-tankers and the rest, whose vested interest is in devising ever more elaborate schemes for talking about reform, cannot acknowledge such a challenge

because it negates their role and undermines the demand for
their product, which is 'politics' itself. The alternative is to
leave the field open to groups such as conservative Christians
who have strong core beliefs on a number of issues which
they can use to generate a great deal of political response.
The simplicity of that appeal and the concentration of
politics on these issues, which previously were seen and
understood as private issues frequently decided on free votes
in Parliament, will Americanise British and European
politics. Preventing this kind of development and moral
polarisation is a key challenge for secular political thinkers
and activists.

The race question

In terms of world position the multiple identities of the
British people are questioned when allegiance or even
connection to other states or religions which are seen to be in
conflict with the UK challenges an idea of loyalty. This has
been most obvious in recent years in the debate over the
'loyalty' of British Muslims during the war on terror. The
three main ways in which British identity has changed are
immigration, elitism and the class system. These areas raise
questions about what it means to be British. Who is
included? Who is excluded? Who would have power? Three
broad positions can be identified: liberal assimilationist,
monoculturalist, and their synthesis in liberal Powellism – a
form of illiberal liberalism.

The liberal assimilationist position, associated with Roy
Jenkins and others, was concerned with the management of
race relations through integration, as Jenkins put it when
Home Secretary:

'Integration' is perhaps a loose word. I do not regard it as meaning the loss, by immigrants, of their own characteristics and culture. I do not think we need in this country a 'melting pot', which will turn everybody out in a common mould, as one of a series of carbon copies of someone's misplaced version of the stereotyped Englishman. I define integration, therefore, not as a flattening process of assimilation but as equal opportunity, accompanied by cultural diversity, in an atmosphere of mutual tolerance.[9]

Powellism articulated a monocultural vision of Britain in which integration was impossible so immigration had to be stopped and perhaps even reversed. There was an acceptance that the presence of immigrants within the community when they were people of colour had to be designated as a 'problem' which needed a 'solution'. Set against this was an inclusive multiculturalism that set out to celebrate diversity and present immigration as an opportunity. For their part, questions of power and the class system were answered by a neo-liberal critique which demanded greater social mobility through, for example, choice in education but which rejected egalitarianism. Though frequently politically aligned with the Powellite position the libertarian position, which opposes the regulation of private life, is in fact diametrically opposed to it, which is ironic of course because Enoch Powell was the first neo-liberal to openly break ranks over the Conservative Party's endorsement of the Attlee settlement.

It is important to separate two dimensions of the identity question. In the broader area the British model of multiculturalism has been significantly more successful over the last thirty years than other European models, for example the French. However, aspects of British policy have been uneven in their application and the temptation for British politicians to use immigration and related issues as a populist issue on which to appeal to the little-England constituency remains powerful. Its most recent and most successful application was in Labour's 1997 general election campaign. The terms of the debate in the UK have been revolutionised by the bizarre marriage of cosmopolitan assimilation and Powellism in a new consensus.

World power and identity flow together because the end of empire, the reorientation towards Europe and the continuing closeness to the USA all have direct repercussions on British identity. In turn the impact of the European Union on the relationship between the constituent parts of the UK has been profound. Much of the analysis of British culture by declinists such as Correlli Barnett has proved to be myopic. Rather than a dependent mass unable to compete in the knowledge economy, the welfare state produced a richer, healthier, more usefully educated population, who have built the fifth largest economy in the world – depending on exchange rates perhaps the fourth. Powellites can accept some of this but have traditionally argued that the cost has been the dilution of the race, of what makes Britain different, and the creation of a yob culture. There are two connected illusions in this: first, that a monocultural Britain ever existed; second, that it is somehow a sign of decay that we now spend more time watching Hollywood movies than listening to *The Archers*, more time cheering David Beckham than applauding *Peter Grimes*. We never did listen to Britten in anything like the numbers that attended games in the old Division One. The great con trick of cultural elitism is the idea that Britten matters on some absolute scale more than Beckham. British creative success since the Festival of Britain in a range of fields from the popular to the elitist has demonstrated that there is no artistic basis for the idea of a decline in British culture. The British people and their culture are more interesting now than in 1940, more united than in

1970 and more self-confident than in 1990. They are more interesting because of immigration, increased secularism and the sophisticated tolerance these slowly bred as they created multiculturalism. Their dynamism and confidence make a nonsense of the cultural critique of the decline of Britain in the works of Martin Wiener or the journalism of Simon Heffer and Roger Scruton.

Furthermore, the image of a public-school-educated liberal elite squandering the inheritance of the Industrial Revolution in the pursuit of a romantic, agrarian and pastoral dream is a stubbornly repeated idea that persists to an extent today. The idea that the way in which the British public school system was created was anti-entrepreneurial, anti-technocratic, anti-scientific in its instincts is entrenched. It was this system, the declinists argue, that created generations of aristocratic people whose idea of success was to own a large landed estate rather than invest capital in enterprise. To join the aristocracy becomes and is the defining destination and definition of success; therefore the dream of success is a house in the country, rather than a larger or more efficient factory. This pervades other areas of society and defines us as anti-entrepreneurial and anti-capitalist. If this cultural declinist thesis were correct then the younger sons of successful businessmen should all become gentlemen, gentleman farmers and gentlemen scholars, and not run factories. As William Rubinstein has shown there is no empirical basis for the argument that the sons of industrialists were educated out of the habit of enterprise.[10]

But more than this, getting rid of an empire was a major modernisation project brought off better by the UK than by any comparable imperial power. Joining the EEC gave recognition to our geographical position, as much as the status of chicken tikka masala as the national dish suggests the place of history in our national identity. To be British is to be local (European) and global (African, Caribbean and Asian).

This generally positive picture, and, I believe, the possibility of a consensus around the creation of a tolerant multicultural society, is undermined by the nature of the political consensus that has been constructed from Thatcherism by the Blair–Brown governments on issues of immigration and asylum. Tony Blair's cultural politics endorse an essentially defensive posture towards British culture that is detrimental to the sustaining of the cultural dynamism which has made Britain a much more civilised place in which to live over the last few decades. It is also dangerous. It is in these respects that world power position and identity combine most directly.

New Labour have abandoned universalism in welfare provision where they can. They have accentuated the strain in Labour Party thinking that has always been concerned with the delivery of benefits to its own constituency of British people who continue to prefer to describe themselves as the white working class. In its immigration and asylum policy it is responding to the most hysterical kind of fears of the other. The economic vision of post-decline Britain accepts a small underclass as the price worth paying for general affluence. The cultural vision of New Labour's Britain accepts the presentation of people fleeing persecution as a threat that needs to be dealt with in order to demonstrate toughness. There are walls and security fences around the contented to protect them from the underclass. There are walls and security fences around Britain to protect us from the migrants.

The construction of walls and the characterisation of asylum seekers as an enemy within are profoundly threatening to the future of our society. It is vital that social democracy has an inbuilt sense of international and global purpose and is not merely concerned with constructing a successful society within the boundaries of a nation state and in the interests of a narrow constituency. This is not merely a moral imperative, but a political necessity: it is simply no longer possible to construct a successful nation state behind walls of monoculturalism.

The fear of economic migration leads to the construction of walls around people who are meant to be the citizens of the democratic, liberal and capitalist world to exclude those who are not. It is the global manifestation of J. K. Galbraith's structure of the domestic economy. These walls are the reason that the West is not seen as the answer to the problems of much of the developing world. Sometimes aid is tossed over the walls, sometimes missiles. This is central to Britain and America's current problem with the pursuit of global war on terrorism. By articulating a democratic citizenship that is exclusive, the West has ensured that it cannot be welcomed as a liberator in places such as Iraq. The walls around social democracy at home are wrong because of the message that they send out about inclusion and exclusion from citizenship, both within the polity and across the communities that are connected to this polity. Multiculturalism is not something of the future but something that is here now. Kinship and political groupings span national, regional and international boundaries through information technology and the media as surely as do brands. A politics which attempts to isolate certain sections of a community and brand them as alien, as unwelcome economic migrants and bogus asylum seekers, is a politics that will alienate significant sections of those that are included as citizens already and reinforce the global sense of two camps. You cannot reassure British Muslims that they are not considered part of a security problem if you suggest the building of concentration camps in rural areas to hold people who are often fleeing fundamentalism in pursuit of freedom in the West.

A social democracy that lacks a sense of internationalism or merely constructs walls around its own polity to defend its culture of contentment is inviting attack. Fortress Britain is a self-image that can no longer be sustained and is no longer compatible with a defence of freedom. It is the aspect of Thatcherism that I most wish New Labour had not taken to heart. That they felt compelled to do so reflects the polarised nature of the times in a wider sense than the narrow concerns of UK domestic politics. In introducing a draconian asylum system and using the language of race politics to discuss asylum seekers, New Labour has reflected a strong aspect of the contemporary consensus.

6

Conclusions: so what?

I do an exercise with my postgraduate students at Kingston in the early stages of their masters or doctoral degrees. After getting them to state clearly and succinctly the thesis for their research, I ask, 'If everything you say in your thesis is true, so what?' My own answer to this question will reflect an underlying tension you will have noticed in this book. Am I describing a Britain in which the decline debate has ended because the country has changed out there in the world of making and doing, or am I describing a Britain in which the decline debate has ended in our own heads and in the conversations we have with each other about what things mean – our discourses? I think we have certainly ended the debate in our heads, except perhaps in the racial dimension of the question of our identity. I certainly do not think that all our real world problems are solved, but they have been changed and we need to give urgent recognition to this. Indeed in ending these particular debates, we have created new debates about how we are doing as a nation that are just as urgent and important. I wrote this book to encourage a shift onto this new terrain and away from the old. There is a danger in this kind of broadly positive writing that in striving for neatness I have painted over too many cracks. So let me restate my argument briefly and then suggest what I see as the major areas of continuing debate and challenge. After that I want to address a few of the other kinds of critique of New Labour that we have not considered so far, especially the issue of trust. Finally, I want to suggest some of the key

themes in the new arguments about ourselves that I think we
should be having and why these matter now.

The argument

The combination of the Thatcher reforms and their endorsement and adjustment by the Blair–Brown governments has
ended the debate about British decline as it was understood
for much of the post-Second World War period in three areas
most importantly: political economy, identity and culture
and our role in the world.

By 2003 Britain had moved from being a state in which
debate centred in both academic analysis and journalistic
comment on the fundamental weakness of the British
experience to being one in which the national conversation
was confident and forward-looking. The terror attacks of 7/7
and the continued polarisation of debate over the legality and
efficacy of the war in Iraq have not reversed our sense of
confidence and modernity. These events have heightened the
extent to which, sometimes for good and sometimes for ill,
the United Kingdom now stands as the economic, cultural
and political first among equals in the European Union, in
terms of economic power, support from a range of member
countries and closeness of the relationship with the United
States. This moment, like all historical moments, will pass.
Circumstances, positions and attitudes will change. There are
new leaders and perhaps we are already, at the time of
writing, seeing the makings of a new economic downturn. But
the mood in which this nation faces such a downturn and the
lives its people lead, whatever happens next, will improve
through confidence in our institutions. That mood will
feature a celebration of our culture and our diversity and a
realisation that this is a dynamic political culture with an
adaptive state and an immensely creative people, capable of

change and reinvention in astonishingly short periods of time and in the face of massive threats. There will be new debates about Britain's position in the world and there will be periods of uncertainty and instability but they will have new causes and different consequences.

The great decline debate was about British identity and culture, economic performance and world position and the way in which these three were interconnected. In terms of British culture, the declinists of the right argued that our public school system had trained enterprise and competitiveness out of our elite. Those of the left argued that this elite failed to build a developmental state. Both agreed that there was something called a 'national' culture and that it could be changed and manipulated by public policy choices to be more or less successful. Also, both argued that the British state was slow to react to change, inefficient for significantly different kinds of reasons and less successful than other states. Though the list of other states we should have resembled varied, there was a clear sense that it was better 'over there'. From the general culturalist perspective there developed a five-strong list of key economic problems:

1. economic growth
2. productivity in manufacturing
3. industrial relations
4. private enterprise
5. public ownership and public services.

In terms of our position in the world the major problem was which of Churchill's three circles should drive our policy – Atlantic, European or Empire/Commonwealth. In terms of identity there were three kinds of problem:

1. the national question
2. the lifestyle/sexuality question
3. the race question.

Across almost all these issues it was the Blair–Brown governments that ended the decline debate as a discourse. It was the combination of the Blair–Brown governments and the legacy of Thatcherism that substantially solved these major areas as problems of policy. Margaret Thatcher did not end British decline either as a discourse or as a felt experience, because she presented a strong thesis on all of these questions and this thesis provoked a correspondingly powerful antithesis that fed and extended the debate. Most importantly she failed to understand the centrality of public services in the felt experience of a nation's greatness so that the impact of her reforms was to extend and deepen the sense of a failing state in terms of schools and hospitals rather than to strengthen a sense of running a state that worked.

The nature of the modernisation that Blair–Brown has achieved in the process of ending these debates is substantially different from the modernisations of the Attlee and the Thatcher governments. Both of those projects exhibited the weaknesses described in the work of James C. Scott on high modernist projects in that they assumed greater knowledge and foresight than the subjects of the projects and the victims they created. This is not to suggest that the Blair–Brown governments have perfected a victimless methodology for implementing political change. Rather, their projects take seriously the consultative aspects of reforming institutions and this concern curtails their ambition and sense of what is doable while ensuring that significant numbers have not suffered the short- or long-term consequences of their policies. The heart of their ability to govern in this way, especially in the period 1997–2003, can be described either as a substantial failure of will and belief, as it is by many critics, or as an appropriate and successful humility about what it is possible to change in the contemporary era in the context of globalisation and the EU.

The basis of this approach has been described as triangulation but I prefer the term 'synthesis'.

The three main aspects of the decline debate – political economy, world position and identity – are sub-divided into different areas of policy and discussion. In many of these areas the policy synthesis created by the Blair–Brown governments has been informed by a progressive agenda and can be called a progressive consensus but in other areas, most importantly racial aspects of the debate about identity, it is much more reactionary in tone and content. In each of these areas new problems and debates have developed, especially after 2003 and the invasion of Iraq, but in none of these areas has the debate returned to the old discourses of failure, decline, decay, ungovernability or hopelessness that characterised so much of the 1970s–1990s. In most of these areas the debate is now about how to progress, how to grow more, how to lead Europe better, how to forge a greater sense of collective identity and so on, rather than on whether it is possible to achieve these objectives. Therefore, I conclude that we live in a new age in which the historical discourses of the last three decades should be put firmly but politely in their place.

So what if everything I say is true? That would mean that we are spending a significant amount of our time discussing the wrong issues in the political debates we are having in this country. That I might be right and this does not matter in the least is another possible answer because the conversations we are having are those that the most important group of voters, the ones who actually turn out, like us having.

There are some problems that our political class, especially in the media, remain obsessed by that are largely irrelevant to the lived experience of the British people in the first decade of the twenty-first century. These include the status of the pound as an independent currency, the future of the United Kingdom and the defence of the unwritten constitution. Each of these is a hangover from old debates rather than an issue with real purchase on the future. The currency issue is one of economic performance rather than national identity or status. The future of the union is made daily more obsolete by globalisation, the deepening of the EU and the mobility of the digital generation. The defence of the unwritten constitution is rendered arcane by legal harmonisation and the profound democratic deficit that existing institutions allow. If this misplaced emphasis on the wrong issues is true, it represents a significant political opportunity for leaders willing to talk through and over the mainstream media directly to people who live their lives in a context that challenges many of the preconceived political wisdoms of the age. I have suggested some of the policy areas that feel irrelevant to significant parts of the contemporary electorate – the pound and the union being the two most striking examples. The political problem is that the electorate as measured by those who actually turn out to vote is getting older and older. Figure 6.1 shows the decline in voter turnout and projects the way in which this problem is going to get worse over time.

The turnout problem: low and unequal

Lewis Baston of the Electoral Reform Society was recently asked to project some thoughts about the shape and nature of elections forward to the year 2025.[1] His first chart projected voter turnout forward twenty years based on his assumptions of social and demographic trends. He assumes that there will be a continued slow deterioration in turnout rather than another 'abrupt fall' as happened in 2001. He goes on to argue that turnout matters in and of itself as 'the glue that binds the citizens of a representative democracy together'. But more significantly he notes: 'Turnout has become unevenly distributed. Research in the 1970s and before, by contrast, found that the effect of social class on turnout was too small to be detectable. A gap started to open up in 1987 and it has become progressively wider since then.' Table 6.1 shows the differing levels of turnout by social class and age in 2005.

Figure 6.1: Turnout in general elections

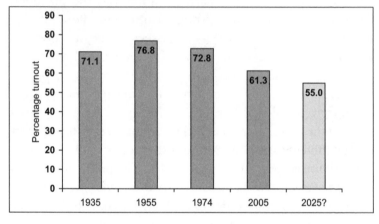

Table 6.1: Turnout by social class and age, 2005 general election

	Turnout %	Change Since 2001	Con % vote	Lab % vote	Lib Dem % vote
Overall	61	+2	33	36	23
Social Class					
AB	71	+3	37	28	29
C1	62	+2	37	32	23
C2	58	+23	33	40	19
DE	54	+1	25	48	18
Age					
18–24	37	-2	28	38	26
25–34	49	+3	25	38	27
35–44	61	+2	27	41	23
45–54	65	0	31	35	25
55–64	71	+2	39	31	22
65+	75	+5	41	35	18

Source: MORI post-election survey, 2005

Baston's research on voter turnout has shown:

> Once a social group has become identified as prone to
> abstention, a vicious circle can set in which is extremely
> difficult to break. Norms and expectations within the group,
> once abstentionism has passed a critical point, will become
> progressively more hostile to participation. Politicians, whose
> rational self-interest will always be to appeal to those groups
> who do turn out and vote, will increasingly neglect the claims
> of non-voting groups, who can then legitimately claim that
> the political system is ignoring their interests. Those members
> of low-turnout groups who have kept voting will become
> disillusioned and stop voting because politics is not relevant
> to their interests.

The political consequences of this trend if it continues are
potentially serious. Voters tend to be middle-class home
owners, which means that elections understate Labour's
'real' level of support. Baston goes on:

> If each constituency had the same voting patterns as in 2005,
> but equal turnout, Labour's lead would have been 5 points
> rather than 3 (although there would be no difference in the
> outcome in terms of seats). Taking into account turnout
> differences within constituencies, equalised turnout would
> have meant a Labour lead of 9 points or so, and a majority of
> over 100 because higher turnout in low-turnout subsections
> of constituencies would tip some over to Labour. Labour is
> only competitive given demographic and turnout trends
> because it has broadened its appeal. In 1964 Wilson's Labour
> struggled to get over 10 per cent of the AB vote, while in 2005
> Blair's party scored 28 per cent.

In many ways these numbers substantiate the Galbraith
thesis of the culture of contentment. If government behaves
in rational vote-maximising ways then it should follow the

groups most likely to vote. If these are higher-income groups in more affluent areas then policies will focus even more intensely on the centre than the classic Downsian model, in which parties centralise in search of the median voter,[2] would have predicted. As Baston argues:

> Governments pursuing policies that increase inequality can do so blatantly, while the pursuit of equality requires a certain amount of discretion. Even when there is this goodwill, turnout differentials can lead to a perception that political actions affecting disadvantaged communities are essentially about *us* doing something for *them* rather than something being done by the community as a whole. Any future right-wing government may find itself able to shift the political territory far to the right.

The evidence on turnout is substantiated by the figures Baston cites on voting age of population (see Figure 6.2).

Figure 6.2: Composition of voting age of population and voters

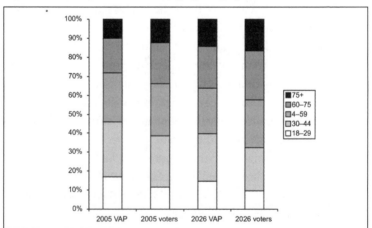

Above and beyond the socio-economic make-up of likely voters there is the age breakdown. As Baston puts it: 'In 2005

the over-60s accounted for 28 per cent of the voting-age population (VAP), but 34 per cent of those voting because of their higher propensity to turn out.' Baston concludes that because of this age imbalance,

> if turnout remains the same in 20 years' time among each age group, demographic change will result in a radical shift in the composition of the voting population. The 2026 census projection suggests that the over-60s proportion of the VAP will rise to 36 per cent, and of those actually voting to 42 per cent. By contrast, the under-40s cast 38 per cent of votes in 2005, but on unchanged turnout patterns will account for only 33 per cent by 2026. A 4-point lead for the under-40s now will become a 9-point lead for the over-60s by 2026. However, it is likely that turnout patterns will change because the initial assumption is that the difference is all life-cycle and no cohort. Today's 25-year-olds are 2026's 45-year-olds, so it seems likely that the presently relatively healthy turnout among the middle-aged will deteriorate as the cohort made up by the current generation of abstainers moves through the life-cycle. Unless something is done, or a most unlikely spontaneous revival in voting among young people takes place, it is possible that nearly half the votes in the 2025 election will be cast by those aged over 60. There are consequences for intergenerational equity in terms of what the political process can deliver, with an ageing population and a strong turnout skew towards older voters. This might be seen in the allocation of public sector resources (with older voters having a stronger political claim on material benefits), pensions of course, in housing and planning policy (the voice of older voters in areas of planned growth will be stronger than that of the under-housed younger non-voters) and culturally (older voters are more likely to be white than younger non-voters). The difference between population and

VAP, and those actually voting, can hardly *but* distort policy and increase inequality to a greater and greater degree through 2025.

If Baston is even half right in this prognosis and if political parties do nothing to alter the way in which they carry out politics, the pressure to keep the political focus on the same tired issues dominating the decline debate will be over-whelming. The political consequence of this narrow focus will be an ever-greater emphasis on issues that are largely irrelevant to significant numbers of younger people, thereby ensuring that fewer and fewer of them vote. So it may be that everything I have said in this book is true on the level of discourse and analysis but will mean nothing in terms of politics because parties will chase the grey vote to the centre and to the issues of the past. In turn these issues will be largely symbolic and ritual in their meanings rather than about life as it is lived.

The ageing electorate and the extent to which politics is about their conversation rather than about the concerns of a majority of people in this country point to an uncomfortable reality. The epochal defeat of the left by Margaret Thatcher in the 1980s opened the way for the reinvention of social democracy on social market lines, which in turn allowed for the creation of a new political consensus around core ideas. But the changes described in this book are also generational. The politically conscious people now coming to maturity did not experience the 1960s and the 1970s. The British disease is not for them stagflation or trade union militancy so much as our inability to win a major football trophy or make a decent sitcom – though even here some progress and grounds for optimism have been found in recent years. More importantly they are not wedded to ideology, nor fetishistic about the form of parliamentary democracy. Rather they are driven by results, league tables and performance. Belief is still central to the identity of their politics – one of the major mistakes of the Demos analysis of the mid-1990s, in works with such evocative titles as *Life after Politics*, was that it took the notion of depoliticisation too far – but the nature of that belief and therefore the measures of success that our own citizens will apply to their governments have changed.[3]

My aim in this book has been to put the Blair–Brown governments into some kind of historical perspective with respect to the period since 1945 in relation to the decline debate. I have argued that they have ended the debate. Blair–Brown have also benefited from and in some ways enhanced twenty years of economic, social and cultural change that rendered 'decline' meaningless as a description of contemporary Britain. But they have done this in such a way that significant progressive possibilities have been closed off. A number of reactionary strains in British culture have been made mainstream. Summing up an era is not easy, especially when the outcome of the next general election is much less predictable than it was ten years ago. The New Labour era has been both much as we thought it was going to be and so very different. Broadly, domestic policy in most areas has gone largely in the direction that we might have anticipated: economic competence, mild constitutional reform and a shift in welfare provision away from universalism have all been delivered in the context of much greater economic stability than I think we would have imagined possible. The minimum wage, family tax credits and consistently low unemployment have produced significant changes in social and economic status for millions of people, and the strength of the performance in areas such as youth unemployment is now rather taken for granted.

It is impossible to satisfy people in some areas of policy. There can never be a health service which is good enough for every conceivable need and there can never be an education system that delivers everything that every parent wants. However, on balance, both sectors have improved in their delivery of frontline services and though the challenge of public sector management has not yet been solved, the public sector is now at the centre of the new political consensus which governs what is possible in British politics. A mainstream social democratic government with a stronger market orientation than previous Labour administrations has buried the issue of Labour's economic competence and re-established it as a party of government. Contemporary views of Labour's record here have been broadly positive. All of this was fairly predictable. What none of us saw coming was Labour's foreign policy. The cause of humanitarian intervention, the response to 9/11 and the Afghanistan and Iraq wars gradually came to dominate British politics. Contemporary views of Labour's performance in foreign policy have been broadly negative. My current instinct is that history will judge the New Labour era in exactly the reverse way.

What about corruption? What about Iraq?

If there is a deep consensus on domestic policy and an emerging consensus on world position, with the extremes excluded, then why do elections matter? With Gordon Brown now Prime Minister and Labour recovering ground in the polls, the outcome of the next general election is uncertain. The non-Labour left or extreme left have always regarded governments of either major party, or indeed any democratically elected government, as pointless, so it is not surprising that they argue that there is no difference between a 'New Conservative' and a New Labour administration. What is striking is the extent to which this attitude is prevalent within the Labour Party itself. Labour's left wing seem to have forgotten what a Tory goverment can be like. Membership of the Labour Party has fallen dramatically since 2003. In the context of the falling turnout, an ageing electorate and a concentration on middle-class floating voters in marginal constituencies, this collapse in the party is likely to bottom out but not reverse in the run-up to the next election. The roots of the decline in party activism lie primarily in the period since 2003 and centre on two issues – trust and Iraq.

Going into politics is a bizarre thing to do with your life and your time. You must be vain, ambitious and all the rest. But what is striking is not how corrupt, in the usual sense of the word (taking money for personal gain; breaking rules to advance yourself), members of the Blair–Brown governments have been, but rather how collectively corrupt they have been: taking money for party gain; breaking rules to advance party, government or ideology. In my view this includes the way that Blair sold the country on the war in Iraq. The greatest lie the British people have been told about foreign policy since 1945 came not from Blair but from Anthony Eden. Blair misled people about the basis for intervention in Iraq by taking, like a good barrister, what he thought were the best arguments the available facts could support rather than the true arguments. At no point did he say we were going to do one thing and then do another. Eden, however, lied from beginning to end about what he was doing and why he was doing it. And for Eden, as Anthony Nutting long ago showed, it was personal.[4]

Was it personal for Blair? Did he potentially wreck the New Labour project, his standing in the world and the future of the Labour Party because he was personally affronted by Saddam Hussein or because he had suddenly become the poodle of George W. Bush, the oil industry and the military-industrial complex? Was he these things all along? I do not believe that he was. The impact of the Iraq War has been so profound that many people have radically changed their minds over the last four years about Blair and New Labour. In a sense, of course, this is the natural process of political change over time, and the Blair–Brown project was remarkably successful for a remarkably long period at keeping a broad national coalition in place supporting its policies.

In the course of my work I have met quite a few politicians. Most of them have been pretty normal people. Some were brighter than others, all were more articulate than most other people I have met, and all had an overt kind of self-belief, even if this obviously, for most, covered up considerable insecurity. One politician who differs from the rest is Michael Foot, because he is a strong poet among politicians and a great writer. But, putting him to one side, most politicians are pretty much like other people. In other words, they do things for complicated and sometimes contradictory reasons that do not always make sense to themselves, and they then feel compelled to justify their actions in ways that make them seem coherent. All of this is obvious, but I think it is too quickly forgotten by both the politicians, who like to appear omnipotent, and their critics, who grant them that omnipotence by the way in which they critique their actions. If the politicians do not actually have the rational and worked-out basis for their actions that their critics assume, then the nature of the world view from which the criticism emerges is immediately rendered obsolete.

So do politicians and journalist critics just need each other? Perhaps. But rather, I would say, we need a different kind of debate, one we are never actually going to get because it is in nobody's interests to listen to one another and learn. Having said all this, is it possible to defend New Labour against the charge of sleaze, against the notion that, as Matthew d'Ancona puts it, it has all gone wrong? D'Ancona has argued that in 1997, all the talk was of better 'schools 'n' hospitals'; of a 'Young Country'; even – heaven help us – of 'Cool Britannia'. In the early days, Mr Blair promised to be 'purer than pure', not to be like the 'last lot'; he could shrug off the allegation that he changed government policy in return for a £1 million donation to Labour, merely by asserting that he was a 'pretty straight sort of guy'. Yet, nine years on, his party is mired in allegations that it traded honours for loans, and the PM himself is expected to be interviewed in the near future by Scotland Yard. Deputy Assistant Commissioner John Yates is behaving like a copper confident that he already has at least one witness who will sing like a canary. These are astonishing times for a government that stormed to power promising to make sleaze a thing of the past.[5]

Has this been, as d'Ancona suggests, a corrupt and a corrupting government on a new scale? It depends on whether or not you think there is a difference between personal gain and satisfaction and collective gain and satisfaction. Peter Mandelson, John Prescott and a very few others, by the standards that held during eighteen years of Tory governments, have been caught fulfilling their own needs and, in Mandelson's case, using the power of office in an inappropriate way. Prescott was tacky, but I have not seen evidence that he really abused power. Almost every other charge against New Labour – loans, lying and the rest – relates to things that have been done for the benefit of the party, the government and the project, and no charges were pressed after the loans-for-honours inquiry. Blair's corruption, such as it was, was about keeping power and keeping Labour in the game. Did he get rich? The Blairs would be much better off had they stayed in the law as a barrister double act. Have Brown, Straw, Beckett, Cooper, Balls or the Milibands made any real money out of being in government? Do they have lucrative directorships in the City? In terms of personal gain, these have been clean governments. So if it has not been about material gain but about political gain, does this make any real difference? Have these governments been collectively corrupt and therefore is it wrong to argue that there has been a break in the way in which politics takes place?

Ten years ago, in the conclusion to a collection of essays I was editing called *New Labour in Power*, I argued that New Labour was about power – getting it and then keeping it. I did not grasp the extent to which this also meant projecting it and using it to take the fight to those who might challenge us. There is a continuity in the pursuit of power New Labour used to win the election and the exercise of power once in office that I did not fully grasp before 1997. The consequences have been Blair's wars. Though the explanations given for these wars were sometimes based on indefensible overt falsehoods, the underlying foundation of the policies was securely a social democratic commitment to humanitarian intervention. In other words, for all their wrong moves and mistakes, I don't think these have been personally corrupt politicians.

The last ten years raise an old but important question: is there something in the nature of democratic politics that leads to collective corruption no matter what the intentions of the politicians at the outset; or is there something corrupt about the people who get into democratic politics? The case for defending Blair–Brown against the charges that have been consistently levelled at their honesty would have been easier to make if they had not also launched the governance and standards debates that began, as I discussed earlier, with the Nolan committee. Here the parallels between the end game of the Major government and the end game of Blair's premiership are clear. When John Major launched his 'back to basics' message he was setting himself and his ministers up for intrusive investigations of their personal circumstances. The media do not have the kinds of rights they so often sanctimoniously claim for themselves in terms of the analysis of public figures in their private lives. There is a strong case for better protection of the privacy of people in public roles and often the media create the problem of standards and trust. When politicians seek to legislate or even pontificate on areas of personal morality, however, they should expect their own morality to be analysed in detail. If they take a stand against personal or individual corruption and are then found to be personally corrupt it is very hard to muster any sympathy for them. If this is the case with personal behaviour and personal gain, then it must also be the case with collective behaviour and collective gain. While it does seem that the Blair–Brown governments have been significantly less personally sleazy than their immediate predecessors, it is also the case that they have been substantially more collectively corrupt. As I have argued, while we might understand why this is so (the overwhelming need to hold onto power so as to perform with greater political competence than any previous Labour government), that does not disguise the extent to which the collective corruption of the Blair premiership further undermined people's trust in politicians. In one way this bending and breaking of rules, this adherence to the letter of truth rather than to its spirit, this exhibition of the arrogance of office and the presumption that power makes right, is worse than personal failings or sexual peccadilloes: such corruption corrodes trust in politicians and standards in public life.

What's next?

Matthew d'Ancona has argued:

> Just as the Iron Lady transformed Labour, so he [Blair] has changed the terms of political trade and, whether one likes it

or not, had a huge impact upon the modern Conservative Party. Without Blair, the Cameron phenomenon would be impossible to imagine. Who would have thought that the Tories would make the environment their core issue, lead the campaign against NHS cuts, promise to hug a hoodie? Last week, a senior Labour strategist said to me that he was concerned his party might lose votes on the left to Mr Cameron. The shape of the political landscape has indeed changed beyond recognition.[6]

The period of Labour government since 2003 has been significantly less successful than the period from 1997 to 2003. The Conservative Party has managed to recover under a new leader. So what happens to the Labour Party and its adherence to the new consensus if David Cameron wins the next election? For Gordon Brown, the unfolding tragic elements of his political career would be complete. He will have gained the prize he sought all his adult life and then lost the power that he exercised better than any Chancellor of the last 100 years. Rather than being like John Major – an extended finale to Margaret Thatcher's governments – Brown will have been a full stop to an era. Despite the endless fascination with Brown's personal story, the deeper question now exercising the minds of Labour activists and politicians is what happens in such a scenario to the Labour Party itself. The New Labour project will be over and with it the discipline of power. There are already signs that old ways are returning, that the left of the party smell blood over Iraq and see their chance to regain some of the ground lost over the last twenty years of centre-right dominance.

Labour usually surges to the left after a defeat. Back in 1931 Ramsay MacDonald took a section of the Labour Party into coalition with the Conservatives. For the three years that followed, under the pacifist leadership of George Lansbury, the party flirted with communist-influenced popular-front politics. Clement Attlee's election to the leadership signalled the end of the leftward movement, though the internal power struggles and feuding continued and were picked up again with a vengeance when Labour lost in 1951, a defeat precipitated by the split in the Cabinet. This provoked the first 'classic' period of Labour's internecine warfare, and the 1950s were characterised by prolonged battles on international and defence issues. Then as now our relationship with the United States was at the root of the divisions, which helped keep Labour out of power for thirteen years. The factionalism of the 1950s, Bevanites versus Gaitskellites, morphed into Bennites versus everyone else in the second 'classic' period of division: the 1980s. The party moved to the far left and it took Michael Foot and then Neil Kinnock a decade to bring it back towards the centre – meeting by meeting, clause by clause in prolonged and bloody trench warfare often fought out through the annual conference in front of the television cameras.

Eighteen years out of power, Labour won again in 1997. History is always just a guide and not a road map but the signs are here. The Campaign Group of left-wing Labour MPs argued that the annual party conference, being the sovereign body of the party, should decide the timetable for Blair's retirement. The last time anyone in the Labour Party spoke about conference sovereignty was during the long battles of the 1980s. Attitudes on the war in Iraq have become rather like unilateralism in the 1980s, a leitmotiv of political credibility for leftists. Elements of factionalism are returning. There is a sense that the left is burying weapons ready for the battle to come. But maybe this time it will be different.

Talking to Labour activists in their twenties, as they begin to contemplate opposition for the first time in their politically active lives, I try to describe the nature of the struggle between the hard left and the rest in the 1980s. It is very difficult indeed. There is an electoral rationalism at the heart of contemporary political activism that finds it hard to grasp why many thousands of Labour supporters thought a policy of massive nationalisation, unilateral nuclear disarmament, a siege economy and withdrawal from the European Economic Community was ever going to win an election. It is perhaps this rationalism and a decade of discipline that will save the Labour Party from a prolonged stay in the wilderness. There is also the ideological underpinning of Cameron's Conservatism. At the moment many of these young Labour people are not especially scared of a Conservative government. Perhaps, they say, the progressive consensus can survive a Tory stint and on the environment Cameron looks very good – hence d'Ancona's source suggesting that Labour could even lose votes from the left. The mood music coming out of the Conservative Party is not making them nervous. The very rationalism of New Labour's new generation leads them to a sneaking admiration for Cameron and what he is doing.

The surges to the left after the split in the Labour government in 1931, and after the election defeats of 1951 and 1979, were born of political passion and energy – the two great virtues of the left. They were a response to division and defeat, which basically said, 'OK, we've tried it their way, now let's try it ours.' From these surges of enthusiasm and energy much destruction followed but also much good policy – policy which appeared radical then but is mainstream now (the whole GLC identity politics agenda for example). Without the surge to the left there might not be the kind of political renewal in terms of policy approaches that Labour will need. What might happen is that the rationalism of the current generation of Labour activists will be married to the freedom offered by opposition and a positive repositioning of the party will take place. The nature of this new positioning will be within the terms of reference of the new consensus and will not see a return to the politics of decline, the alternative economic strategy and the debates of the past. Even if the Conservatives do form governments in the next period, they will govern, as I have argued, in the consensus formed by the Blair–Brown administrations.

Last word – the future of liberal intervention and a test of greatness

The radicalism of this progressive consensus on domestic issues and on international policy should not be exaggerated nor understated. In domestic policy, especially in the reform of political structures, timidity in progressive ambition has led to many missed opportunities for bolder change since 1997, an era in which large majorities were wasted in the support of minor tinkering with the structures of power and inequality. By contrast, the rediscovery by the left of the cause of humanitarian intervention, the work of Gordon Brown on Third World debt and the projection of militant democratic power against tyranny will come to be seen as embodying a defining era in the recovery of post-war Britain. The reassertion of Britain's place in the world as a beacon of liberal internationalism and the articulation of an ethical foreign policy which shames the standard positions of most other major European players will in future be seen as the core of the Blair–Brown legacy and a central component of the way in which they ended decline.

Exploring the three main themes of contemporary British history – world position, economy and identity – in a short work such as this entails the editing out of much, especially in terms of the context of international policy. It is important therefore to stress what I am not arguing. I am not suggesting that Britain is in an old-fashioned imperial sense great again. But I am saying that Blair–Brown have harnessed the deployment of British power for humanitarian causes that did not necessarily coincide with narrow realist definitions of British interest. In doing this they have exposed a major division between Labour and old Conservative foreign policy objectives. It is in the area of liberal interventionism, more-over, that we might also see the first source of the potential for greatness in the New Labour governments, though the accompanying record on human rights has been mixed. To evaluate Labour's record on intervention it is important to remember where you are standing when you ask the question. There are many pockets of this globe – East Timor, Kosovo, Kurdistan – where Tony Blair is now and always will be a hero. If you are sitting in a bunker in Baghdad or the detention centre at Belmarsh on the other hand, Blair will seem like a loose cannon who broke international law and reversed what had been a growing place for human rights in the British judicial system.

In pursuing an interventionist foreign policy to achieve humanitarian objectives before 2003, the Labour government was actually performing in ways that were in tune with the British record over the post-war period. When reading works like Correlli Barnett's *The Collapse of British Power* or his *The Lost Peace*, it might be assumed that in the twenty years after 1945 Britain was incapable of the operation of hard military power. In fact the UK launched thirty-four foreign military interventions of varying scale, duration and intensity between 1949 and 1970. These interventions were not merely imperial policing operations of the traditional kind, nor were they launched in defence of economic interests. John Van Wingen and Herbert Tillema, who studied this period of British military intervention, asked themselves whether Britain's extensive post-war military activity can be understood simply as the continuation of great power habits by a state no longer great. The answer is no. The pattern of military intervention is different in important ways from that usually expected of a great power. England practised military intervention primarily within the post-war Empire, upon request and on behalf of constituted authorities, only after the outbreak of violence and in the immediate vicinity of her Army bases. Even within the constraints of time and place intervention did not serve functions often imputed to her past behaviour. She did not systematically use military force in order to retain the Empire, nor to protect trade monopolies, profitable foreign investments, nor overseas citizens.[7]

The way Britain used power, they argued, was to help manage withdrawal from empire and support local authorities in dealing with outbreaks of violence. Britain did not use military power to further obvious national interests but rather to aid new administrations in parts of the post-war empire from which it was withdrawing. In the main the interventions took place because the competent authority requested British military aid. They were based on a clear articulation of a just cause, the defence of local authorities against violence, they were limited to the intentions expressed and they had a good likelihood of success. When launched the force used was proportionate to the task stated and the forces withdrew when the mission was completed. In these ways the military interventions met the tests of just-war theory.[8] Many of these operations have the same policy characteristics and motivations as the military interventions launched by the Blair–Brown governments before 2003 – though these later operations were of course launched by post-imperial Britain and took place in places outside the Commonwealth. In other words, there is considerable continuity between the exercise of military power in the period since 1997 and the tradition of British military intervention since 1945.

This continuity suggests that the parallels between the 1950s and the present era are as strong in foreign policy as I have argued they are in domestic. The major difference between then and now is in the attitude of conservative isolationist opinion – across all three political parties – to the issue of intervention and to the way in which this connects to Britain's role in the world. This is the element of the Blair–Brown consensus that was most at risk from a change of leadership and even more from a change of government.

The foreign policy of the Blair–Brown governments, where it has been concerned with humanitarian disasters, has been consistently progressive. That is, it has attempted to give substance to the idea of an ethical foreign policy as articulated by Robin Cook in the early part of the New Labour era. At the heart of Cook's call for an ethical basis for foreign policy was the idea that it should be different from a conservative or reactionary foreign policy. It should be different because it should be based on universalist principles rather than simple expressions of national interest. A conservative or reactionary foreign policy is one that will place national interest always and everywhere above anything else. If we believe that this is the beginning and the end of the foreign policy question then we should accept that the attempt to construct an ethical foreign policy is impossible. At the heart of a progressive foreign policy is the victim of gross human rights violations, wherever that victim is found. We shape a progressive foreign policy by being forthright about our victim-centred approach to the world. This idealist basis for policy represents a marked break with the realist basis of Margaret Thatcher and John Major's foreign policy and it has not by any means functioned across the board. There is, for example, no way in which a major arms-manufacturing nation can be in the business of exporting small arms and stop those arms fuelling conflicts. Nor can a government that is trying to reduce unemployment turn its back on substantial large-scale arms deals. Yet these national interests have not determined the major landmarks of New Labour's foreign policy since 1997. In fact the major interventions in East Timor, Kosovo, Sierra Leone, Afghanistan and Iraq were all influenced by an interpretation of global rather than national interests.

It is worth pausing on this question of global interests for a moment as it has long been a challenging one for social democrats. Should social democracy be about building walls around a particular polity to defend it and keep its people safe from various threats? If so, social democrats should argue in support of venturing out from this little island only when material threats exist to its people. So when, for example, civil war breaks out in Yugoslavia they should agree with conservative isolationists that the best course of action is to do nothing. They should also agree with left-wing isolationists that the best course of action for the Iraqi people is that we should leave them living under a genocidal dictator. And today they should be arguing hard against any form of intervention against the government of Sudan with respect to its policy in Darfur. There was no argument for a unique and vital British national interest in any of these cases. The argument that Blair articulated in support of these policies was profoundly important for understanding one of the major dimensions of the new age in which we now live; in his recent articulation of the case in Los Angeles Blair wove the different strands together:

> What are the values that govern the future of the world? Are they those of tolerance, freedom, respect for difference and diversity or those of reaction, division and hatred? . . . Unless we reappraise our strategy, unless we revitalise the broader

global agenda on poverty, climate change, trade and, in respect of the Middle East, bend every sinew of our will to making peace between Israel and Palestine, we will not win. And this is a battle we must win. What is happening today out in the Middle East, in Afghanistan and beyond, is an elemental struggle about the values that will shape our future. It is in part a struggle between what I will call Reactionary Islam and Moderate, Mainstream Islam. But its implications go far wider. We are fighting a war, but not just against terrorism but about how the world should govern itself in the early twenty-first century, about global values. The root causes of the current crisis are supremely indicative of this. Ever since September 11th, the USA has embarked on a policy of intervention in order to protect its and our future security. Hence Afghanistan. Hence Iraq. Hence the broader Middle East initiative in support of moves towards democracy in the Arab world. The point about these interventions, however, military and otherwise, is that they were not just about changing regimes but changing the values systems governing the nations concerned. The banner was not actually 'regime change', it was 'values change' . . . We could have chosen security as the battleground. But we didn't. We chose values. We said we didn't want another Taleban or a different Saddam. Rightly, in my view, we realised that you can't defeat a fanatical ideology just by imprisoning or killing its leaders; you have to defeat its ideas . . . it is almost incredible to me that so much of Western opinion appears to buy the idea that the emergence of this global terrorism is somehow our fault. For a start, it is indeed global. No one who ever half-bothers to look at the spread and range of activity related to this terrorism can fail to see its presence in virtually every major nation in the world. It is directed at the USA and its allies, of course. But it is also directed at nations who could not conceivably be said to be allies of the West. It is also rubbish to suggest that it is the product of poverty. It is true it will use the cause of poverty. But its fanatics are hardly the champions of economic development. It is based on religious extremism. That is the fact. And not any religious extremism; but a specifically Muslim version . . . This is not just about security or military tactics. It is about hearts and minds, about inspiring people, persuading them, showing them what our values at their best stand for . . . Though left and right still matter in politics, the increasing divide today is between open and closed. Is the answer to globalisation protectionism or free trade? Without hesitation, I am on the open side of the argument. The way for us to handle the challenge of globalisation is to compete better, more intelligently, more flexibly. We have to give our people confidence we can compete. See competition as a threat and we are already on the way to losing . . . This struggle is one about values. Our values are worth struggling for. They represent humanity's progress throughout the ages and at each point we have had to fight for them and defend them. As a new age beckons, it is time to fight for them again.[9]

This speech sums up the distance we have travelled from Stalin asking about the Pope's divisions; as Blair says, the current conflicts are about values as much as missiles. We are now in a conflict about values, against an enemy that is not only a state but also a network of networks. The test of greatness for a nation in such a conflict is therefore measured across the range of what it does at home and abroad.

Critics of the Blair–Brown foreign policy argue that rather than it being progressive or value led, as Blair put it in Los Angeles, it is conservative. A conservative foreign policy is one that expresses national interest in terms beyond just security but includes the economic interest of a broad entity called the West. Therefore a conservative will pursue intervention on the basis of the control of resources such as oil because of the pressing political and economic need to deliver stable supplies. These critics would argue that the real motivation for the Blair–Brown foreign policy, however, is the economic interests of the UK and its allies. Critics also suggest that the current policy is reactionary because the UK will act unilaterally or, more often, work hard to stop collective action through the United Nations when it does not see vital economic or strategic gains for the UK. But in the Los Angeles speech and elsewhere, Blair made it clear that he preferred to act through the structures of the United Nations. Indeed, ideally, a progressive foreign policy should be conducted through the United Nations and in line with international law and international humanitarian law. I say 'ideally' because it can be argued that the responsibility to protect and the rights of victims to be saved from gross violations of human rights are more important in certain circumstances that the mechanisms of international law or the procedures of the United Nations. The case of preventing genocide in Kosovo substantiated this. On that occasion it was NATO with a broad coalition of support that acted to stop a renewal of ethnic cleansing. Many argue, however, that without UN sanction the intervention in Kosovo was illegal. The intervention in Iraq, critics maintain, fell on every measure of what should constitute a progressive foreign policy because it was an illegal, unilateral act taken for economic motivations in the interests of Western imperial powers.

There is some truth in these charges against the intervention in Iraq. The intervention should have been based on a second resolution. Though the legal basis in terms of material breach of UN resolutions stretching back to 1991 could have been made more powerfully and the UN Convention on Genocide could have been invoked, they were not. Instead the UK and US governments relied on the issue of WMD and thereby discredited not just that intervention but the cause of liberal intervention and the battle for values much more widely. The question for the future is how we are going to continue to fight the war of values that Brown said in his first interview as Prime Minister is necessary in the years to come. The lessons of the Blair–Brown foreign policy up to 2003 suggest that it is possible to shape a progressive foreign policy. Ideally we do this by putting victims first, by understanding our national interest in terms of promoting, protecting and enforcing human rights around the world and by working through the mechanisms of international law and the United Nations. Then we come up against cases in the real world which challenge this model. For Blair and Brown the challenge that came along was Iraq. That challenge left the ethical foreign policy in tatters. The new challenge, in Darfur, is another opportunity to try to fit the policy back together and reforge the consensus, because we all agree that gross human rights violations in Darfur should be stopped. The question is how.

The government of Sudan has been fighting rebel groups in the Darfur region of the country for several years. The government employ militia groups called the Janjaweed to kill civilians, rape and kidnap women and burn villages. The African Union force that has pushed the Janjaweed back does not have enough money or equipment to do its job properly. It does not have planes to enforce the no-fly zone. It is constantly being attacked by the rebels and by the government's militia. The best option is for a United Nations force to replace the AU peacekeepers. But this is the real dilemma the UN system faces us with. Resolutions have authorised the sending of a peacekeeping force to the Darfur region. That force cannot go to Darfur unless the Khartoum government agrees to their entry. The government of Sudan is a coalition and not an Islamic government. It is targeting its African population in Darfur and consistently breaking agreements. The rebels fighting the government who did not sign the peace agreement have committed their own atrocities. It is worth noting that all the perpetrators and all the victims in this conflict are Muslims. A recent Human Rights Watch (HRW) report stated that the government was indiscriminately bombing civilian-occupied villages in the rebel-held north of Darfur. The report quoted HRW's Africa director as saying, 'Government forces are bombing villages with blatant disregard for civilian lives. A penalty for indiscriminate bombing in Darfur is UN Security Council sanctions, which should be imposed now.' But would the imposition of sanctions make the deployment of a UN force more or less likely?

The HRW report went on:

> Firsthand sources report flight crews rolling bombs out of the back ramps of Antonovs, a means of targeting that was often practised by government forces in their 21-year civil war with rebels in southern Sudan. This method is so inaccurate that it cannot strike at military targets without a substantial risk of harm to civilians. International humanitarian law prohibits such attacks, which can constitute war crimes. Deliberately attacking civilians is in all circumstances prohibited and a war crime. So here is the rub – the government that plans on ethnically cleansing part of its territory as a 'counter-insurgency' operation is the government that can say yes or no to a UN force intervening to stop the genocide.[10]

A progressive response should be that international law needs to be enforced, that the structures exist and need to be used and made to work. That is what was said in Rwanda in 1994. Then the UK, the USA and France blocked intervention. This time the UN has passed resolutions authorising deployment but the government of Sudan has refused to agree the detailed terms of the deployment. In this case there seems to me to be a need to square the circle: some states sacrifice their sovereignty when they fail to protect their own citizens or are indeed themselves attacking their own citizens. The ethical debate for progressives should be about what the threshold of violence should be before a state no longer has the right to agree or disagree to intervention. The International Criminal Court could be the institution that makes such a decision. But this does not then lead to full-scale invasion. There are many measures that can be taken short of that. But any measures taken must be in line with international law or else like Kosovo they will not be repeatable. This is the key – the victim-centred progressive foreign policy we need is one that is permanent, repeatable, enforceable and predictable. Only international law can give us these things and the only way international law can be made to work is if it recognises that some states do not belong in the community of nations.

In his Los Angeles speech Blair outlined the nature of the foreign policy that Britain needs to pursue in this new age. Darfur is the most important contemporary challenge to this new vision for Britain as a world leader in the war of values that is taking place. If the Blair–Brown governments have any potential for being seen as defining governments of a new age then it will be through their ending of the decline debate on domestic issues and through their actions on the world stage. In international policy the new test of greatness will come not only from their actions but also from the articulation of complex convictions that have characterised policy on intervention, anti-terrorism, debt and aid. At the heart of this approach is the basis for a European alternative to hard American power. It is the combination of soft and hard power in the process of encouraging, cajoling and maybe even forcing regional powers to take responsibility for the problems around them that is at the centre of this new policy. The major test of this policy is taking place now in Darfur. It is time for African, Asian and Arab states to join Western states in the battle of values and take the lead in dealing with the unfolding genocide in Darfur. Whether or not these states will abandon their post-colonial alibis for inaction remains to be seen. The UK has awoken from the mesmerising effect of post-imperial guilt to be a force behind the next move in the global war on terror. This next stage in the post-9/11 conflict will entail the linkage between the right to development, the reassertion of international law and continuing efforts to prevent attacks and capture perpetrators with a ever-stronger commitment to democratic values. In order that the next phase of this conflict may build on the successes and leave behind the failures of the first phase, there is considerable work to be done on human rights and on understanding the nature of British identity. The ambition of the Blair–Brown modernisation project was always smaller than that of Attlee or Thatcher but the record of its achievements across domestic and international policy within the terms of this limited ambition has been impressive – long-term economic stability and growth, devolution, welfare to work, liberal interventionism, a lead on Third World debt and combating AIDS and a constructive leadership in Europe.

As the many-headed beast of decline consumes itself, the field of political argument and historical research opens. The notion that Britain should be Number One again is so riddled with contradiction and ambiguity that it has become a hollow and meaningless call. We are at a moment of significant transition from an old world into a new. The UK sits as the leading European power with a successful economy and some degree of social cohesion. The mindsets of the declinologists and the cultural and political weight of our past has lifted. As it lifts it allows light to be shed on the other Britains that have struggled and suffered through the century.

The endings of two other books occur to me as I write the last sentences of this one. The greatest social democratic thinker of the post-war era, Tony Crosland, ended his highly influential study *The Future of Socialism* by considering what socialism, with the problem of production solved and the future about the problem of distribution, might now turn its attention to:

> We need not only higher exports and old-age pensions, but more open-air cafes, brighter and gayer streets at night, later closing hours for public houses, more local repertory theatres, better and more hospitable hoteliers and restaurateurs, brighter and cleaner eating houses, more riverside cafes, more pleasure gardens on the Battersea model, more murals and pictures in public places, better designs for furniture and pottery and women's clothes, statues in the centre of new housing estates, better-designed new street lamps and telephone kiosks and so on ad infinitum.[11]

His desires may seem quaint but only because of the extent to which, across all aspects of domestic policy, we have exceeded his expectations. Meanwhile, at the end of his *English History 1914–1945*, A. J. P. Taylor welcomed the election of the 1945 Labour government: 'Few now sang "Land of Hope and Glory". Few even sang "England Arise". England had risen all the same.'[12] The United Kingdom has arisen and in this dark world with an uncertain future it has not returned to being a land chasing glory but is still a land that offers hope to many who live under tyranny. The politics of the twenty-first century are not for young countries but they are for countries that have national conversations about the future and which understand the moral ambiguities of their role in the bloody passage of the twentieth century. Our dance to the music of decline is finally over.

Notes

Prologue

1. British Council Annual Lecture. www.hm-treasury.gov.uk/
   newsroom_and_speeches/press/2004/press_63_04.cfm

Chapter 1

1. Theodor Adorno, *Notes to Literature*, vol. 1 (New York:
   Columbia University Press, 1991), p. 4.
2. Originally published in 1975. Available in *The Book of Sand
   and Shakespeare's Memory* (London: Penguin, 2001),
   pp. 3–11.
3. Julia Margo and Sonia Sodha, 'State of the Nation 2007:
   Audit', in Julia Margo (ed.), *Beyond Liberty: Is the Future
   of Liberalism Progressive?* (London: Institute of Public
   Policy Research, 2007), p. 83.
4. Peter Hennessy, *Never Again: Britain 1945–51*, 2nd ed.
   (London: Penguin, 2006) and *Having It So Good: Britain in
   the Fifties* (London: Allen Lane, 2006).
5. David Kynaston's *Austerity Britain 1945–51* (London:
   Bloomsbury, 2007) is the first in his four-volume series
   Tales from the New Jerusalem.
6. Polly Toynbee and David Walker, *Did Things Get Better?*
   (London: Penguin, 2001) and *Better or Worse? Has Labour
   Delivered?* (London: Bloomsbury, 2005).
7. Simon Jenkins, *Thatcher and Sons: A Revolution in Three Acts*
   (London: Allen Lane, 2006).
8. See the discussion in Richard English and Michael Kenny,
   'British Decline or the Politics of Declinism', *British Journal
   of Politics and International Relations* (1999), vol. 1,
   pp. 252–66.

9. Martin Weiner, *English Culture and the Decline of the Industrial Spirit 1850–1980* (Cambridge: Cambridge University Press, 1981).

10. Correlli Barnett, *The Collapse of British Power* (London: Eyre Methuen, 1972).

11. See for example B. W. E. Alford, *British Economic Performance 1945–1975* (Basingstoke: Macmillan Education, 1988); Eric Hobsbawm, 'Britain: A Comparative View', in Brian Brivati and Harriet Jones (eds), *What Difference Did the War Make?* (Leicester: Leicester University Press, 1993), pp. 20–33; Michael Dintenfass, *The Decline of Industrial Britain 1870–1980* (London: Routledge, 1992); C. H. Feinstein, 'Production and Productivity 1920–1962', in Derek H. Aldcroft and Peter Fearon (eds), *Economic Growth in Twentieth-Century Britain* (London: Macmillan, 1969); L. J. Williams, *Britain and the World Economy 1919–1970* (London: Fontana, 1971). Important counter-arguments are contained in Jim Tomlinson, 'Welfare and the Economy: The Economic Impact of the Welfare State 1945–1951', *20th Century British History* (1995), vol. 6, pp. 194–219; Jim Tomlinson, 'Inventing Decline: The Falling Behind of the British Economy in the Postwar Years', *Economic History Review* (1996), vol. 49, pp. 731–57.

12. See for example David Marquand, *The Progressive Dilemma: From Lloyd George to Kinnock* (London: Heinemann, 1991); David Marquand, *The New Reckoning: Capitalism, States and Citizens* (Cambridge: Polity Press, 1997); David Marquand, *The Unprincipled Society: New Demands and Old Politics* (London: Jonathan Cape, 1988); Joel Krieger, *Reagan, Thatcher and the Politics of Decline* (Cambridge: Polity Press, 1986); Tom Nairn, *The Break-Up of Britain: Crisis and Neo-nationalism*, 2nd ed. (London: New Left, 1981); Will Hutton, *The State We're In*, rev. ed. (London: Vintage, 1996).

13. Andrew Gamble's discussion of the decline debate is one of the most interesting and he touches on these issues in *Britain in Decline: Economic Policy, Political Strategy and the British State* (Basingstoke: Macmillan, 1981); see also James Raven, 'Viewpoint: British History and the Enterprise

Culture', *Past and Present* (1989), vol. 123, pp. 178–204, which cites David Granick, *Managerial Comparisons of Four Developed Countries: France, Britain, United States, and Russia* (Cambridge, MA & London: MIT Press, 1972); Ronald Dore, *British Factory, Japanese Factory: The Origins of National Diversity in Industrial Relations* (London: Allen & Unwin, 1972); Jean Millar, *British Management versus German Management: A Comparison of Organisational Effectiveness in West German and UK Factories* (Farnborough: Saxon House, 1979).

14. G. C. Allen, *The British Disease: A Short Essay on the Nature and Causes of the Nation's Lagging Wealth* (London: Institute of Economic Affairs, 1976).

15. Ken Coates and Fred Singleton (eds), *The Just Society* (Nottingham: Spokesman, 1977).

16. Peter Hennessy, *Whitehall* (London: Secker & Warburg, 1989).

17. See the two sides of the debate in Keith Robbins, 'British Culture versus British Industry' and W. D. Rubinstein, 'Cultural Explanations for Britain's Economic Decline: How True?', both in Bruce Collins and Keith Robbins (eds), *British Culture and Economic Decline* (London: Weidenfeld & Nicolson, 1989); W. D. Rubinstein, *Capitalism, Culture, and Decline in Britain 1750–1990* (London: Routledge, 1993), pp. 102–39; Correlli Barnett, *Collapse of British Power*, pp. 24–43. See also Correlli Barnett, *The Audit of War: The Illusion and Reality of Britain as a Great Nation* (London: Macmillan, 1986), introduction and final two chapters; Sidney Pollard, *The Wasting of the British Economy: British Economic Policy 1945 to the Present* (London: Croom Helm, 1982), pp. 71–101; Sidney Pollard, 'Education, Science and Technology: Conclusion', in *Britain's Prime and Britain's Decline: The British Economy 1870–1914* (London: Edward Arnold, 1989); Weiner, *English Culture and the Decline of the Industrial Spirit 1850–1980*; Julia Wrigley, 'Technical Education in the Nineteenth Century', in Bernard Elbaum and William Lazonick (eds), *The Decline of the British Economy* (Oxford: Clarendon Press, 1986), pp. 162–87; Dintenfass, *Decline of Industrial Britain 1870–1980*, pp. 59–72.

Chapter 2

1. Brian Brivati, Julia Buxton and Anthony Seldon (eds), *The Contemporary History Handbook* (Manchester: Manchester University Press, 1996).
2. Richard Brent, 'Butterfield's Tories: "High Politics" and the Writing of Modern British Political History', *Historical Journal* (1987), vol. 30, pp. 943–54.
3. Quoted ibid.
4. All quotes in this section are from Brent, 'Butterfield's Tories', pp. 948–51.
5. Quoted in Richard English and Michael Kenny, 'Public Intellectuals and the Question of British Decline', *British Journal of Politics and International Relations* (2001), vol. 3, pp. 274–5.
6. Peter Riddell, *Hug Them Close: Blair, Clinton, Bush and the 'Special Relationship'* (London: Politico's, 2006).
7. Michael Shanks, *The Stagnant Society: A Warning* (Harmondsworth: Penguin, 1961).
8. *The Anatomy of Britain* (London: Hodder & Stoughton, 1962); *The Anatomy of Britain Today* (London: Hodder & Stoughton, 1965); *The New Anatomy of Britain* (London: Hodder & Stoughton, 1971); *The Changing Anatomy of Britain* (London: Hodder & Stoughton, 1982); *The Essential Anatomy of Britain: Democracy in Crisis* (London: Hodder & Stoughton, 1992); *Who Runs This Place?: The Anatomy of Britain in the 21st Century* (London: John Murray, 2004).
9. English and Kenny, 'Public Intellectuals and the Question of British Decline'.
10. Vernon Bogdanor, 'Mad monk's new creed', *Times Higher Education Supplement*, 24 May 2002.
11. Andrew Denham and Mark Garnett, 'From "Guru" to "Godfather": Keith Joseph, "New" Labour and the British Conservative Tradition', *Political Quarterly* (2001), vol. 72, no. 1, pp. 97–106.
12. 'Inflation is Caused by Governments', speech at Preston, 5 September 1974, published in Keith Joseph, *Reversing the Trend: A Critical Re-Appraisal of Conservative Economic and Social Policies* (Chichester: Barry Rose, 1975).

13. Thatcher Archive [fo 7], 5 June 1979, Margaret Thatcher. Off-the-record press briefing after meeting the French President, Valéry Giscard d'Estaing.
14. English and Kenny, 'Public Intellectuals and the Question of British Decline'.
15. Tony Benn, speech at The Crisis of the Left debate, Central Hall, Westminster, 17 March 1980.
16. *Smiley's People*, BBC2, 1982.
17. Nevil Shute, *In the Wet* (London: William Heinemann, 1953).
18. William Woodruff, *The Road to Nab End: A Lancashire Childhood* (London: Eland, 2000).
19. Correlli Barnett, *The Audit of War: The Illusion and Reality of Britain as a Great Nation* (London: Macmillan, 1986).
20. Winston Churchill, *The Second World War*, vol. 1: *The Gathering Storm* (London: Cassell, 1948), ch. 8.
21. For a good overview of Britain's relative position in the twentieth century see David Reynolds, *Britannia Overruled: British Policy and World Power in the Twentieth Century* (London: Longman, 1991).
22. Robert K. Massie, *Dreadnought: Britain, Germany, and the Coming of the Great War* (New York: Random House, 1991).
23. Malcolm Gladwell, *The Tipping Point: How Little Things Can Make a Big Difference* (Boston & London: Little, Brown, 2000).
24. Speech given in San Francisco, 18 September 1967. Transcript available at www.atomicarchive.com.
25. Transcripts of the meetings between Reagan and Mikhail Gorbachev meetings can be found at www.cnn.com/SPECIALS/cold.war/episodes/22/documents/reykjavik.
26. Anders Stephanson, *Manifest Destiny: American Expansionism and the Empire of Right* (New York: Hill & Wang, 1995).
27. Aaron L. Friedberg, *The Weary Titan: Britain and the Experience of Relative Decline 1895–1905* (Princeton: Princeton University Press, 1988).
28. See David Kynaston, *The City of London*, vol. 2: *Golden Years 1890–1914* (London: Chatto & Windus, 1995).

29. See Harold G. Vatter, *The Drive to Industrial Maturity: The U.S. Economy 1860–1914* (Westport, CT: Greenwood Press, 1976) and Donald Cameron Watt, *Succeeding John Bull: America in Britain's Place 1900–1975* (Cambridge: Cambridge University Press, 1984).
30. Geoffrey Warner, 'The Impact of the Second World War upon British Foreign Policy', in Brian Brivati and Harriet Jones, *What Difference Did the War Make?* (Leicester: Leicester University Press, 1993).
31. David Edgerton, *England and the Aeroplane: An Essay on a Militant and Technological Nation* (Basingstoke: Macmillan, 1991); and see Correlli Barnett's trilogy, *The Collapse of British Power* (London: Eyre Methuen, 1972), *The Audit of War* (op. cit.) and *The Lost Victory: British Dreams, British Realities 1945–50* (London: Macmillan, 1995).
32. Edgerton, *England and the Aeroplane*, pp. 80–1.
33. Niall Ferguson, *The Pity of War* (London: Allen Lane, 1998); and Joanna Bourke, *An Intimate History of Killing: Face-to-Face Killing in Twentieth Century Warfare* (London: Granta: 1999).
34. Paul Foot, *The Vote: How It Was Won and How It Was Undermined* (London: Viking, 2006).
35. Amartya Sen, *Identity and Violence: The Illusion of Destiny* (New York: W. W. Norton, 2006).
36. Jean-François Revel, *How Democracies Perish* (London: Weidenfeld & Nicolson, 1985).
37. J. K. Galbraith, *The Culture of Contentment* (London: Sinclair-Stevenson, 1992) – an idea also articulated by Will Hutton.

Chapter 3

1. See the chapters by Harriet Jones and Michael Kandiah in their collection, *The Myth of Consensus: New Views on British History 1945–64* (Basingstoke: Macmillan, 1996).
2. There is a case for using 'settlement' rather than 'consensus' to describe the immediate post-war phase but 'consensus' is the more generally understood term.
3. Andrew Shonfield, *British Economic Policy since the War* (Harmondsworth: Penguin, 1958).

4. Peter Hennessy, *The Prime Minister: The Office and Its Holders since 1945* (London: Allen Lane, 2000); David Marquand, *The New Reckoning: Capitalism, States and Citizens* (Cambridge: Polity Press, 1997); Anthony Sampson, *Who Runs This Place?: The Anatomy of Britain in the 21st Century* (London: John Murray, 2004).

5. James C. Scott, *Seeing like a State: How Certain Schemes to Improve the Human Condition Have Failed* (New Haven, CT: Yale University Press, 1998).

6. Ibid., pp. 2–5.

7. Ibid., p. 343.

8. Ibid., p. 310.

9. Ibid., p. 341.

10. See Michael Foot, 'Introduction', in *Aneurin Bevan*, 1-vol. ed. (London: Victor Gollancz, 1998).

11. See Brian Brivati, 'Woodrow Wyatt', in Greg Rosen (ed.), *Dictionary of Labour Biography* (London: Politico's, 2001).

12. See 'Gordon Brown', in Kevin Jefferys (ed.), *Labour Forces: From Ernie Bevin to Gordon Brown* (London: I. B. Tauris, 2002).

13. See Brian Brivati, *Hugh Gaitskell* (London: Richard Cohen, 2001); Brian Brivati, 'Introduction', in Alan Bullock, *Ernest Bevin*, 1-vol. ed., ed. Brian Brivati (London: Politico's, 2002).

14. See 'Crosland as Apparatnik', in Dick Leonard (ed.), *Crosland and New Labour* (Basingstoke: Macmillan, 1999).

15. See Brian Brivati, 'Desmond Donnelly', in Rosen, *Dictionary of Labour Biography*.

16. David Marquand, *The Unprincipled Society: New Demands and Old Politics* (London: Jonathan Cape, 1988).

17. J. Ramsay MacDonald, *Socialism: Critical and Constructive* (London: Cassell, 1921); Herbert Tracey, *The British Labour Party: Its History, Growth, Policy and Leaders*, 3 vols (London: Caxton, 1948).

18. MacDonald, *Socialism*, reproduced in J. Ramsay MacDonald, *Ramsay MacDonald's Political Writings*, ed. Bernard Barker (London: Allen Lane, 1972), pp. 209–11.

19. Ibid.

20. Herbert Morrison, 'Economic Socialisation', in Tracey, *British Labour Party*, vol. 2, p. 14.

21. Aneurin Bevan, *In Place of Fear* (London: William
    Heinemann, 1952); C. A. R. Crosland, *The Future of
    Socialism* (London: Jonathan Cape, 1956); Hugh Gaitskell,
    The Diary of Hugh Gaitskell 1945–1956, ed. Philip M.
    Williams (London: Jonathan Cape, 1983).
22. Nick Ellison, 'Labour and Welfare Politics', in Brian Brivati
    and Richard Heffernan (eds), *The Labour Party: A
    Centenary History* (Basingstoke: Macmillan, 2000), p. 433.

Chapter 4

1. Lawrence Black, *The Political Culture of the Left in Affluent
   Britain, 1951–1964: Old Labour, New Britain?* (London:
   Palgrave Macmillan, 2003).
2. David Butler and Richard Rose, *The British General Election
   of 1959* (London: Macmillan, 1960).

Chapter 5

1. Robert Cooper, 'The Post-Modern State', in Mark Leonard
   (ed.), *Re-Ordering the World* (London: Foreign Policy
   Centre, 2002), pp. 16–18.
2. Cited in Rogers Brubaker and Frederick Cooper, 'Beyond
   "Identity"', *Theory and Society* (2000), vol. 29, pp. 1–47.
3. Iain Macwhirter, 'The New Morality Party', *Scotsman*, 15 July
   1997.
4. Stephen Timms, 'The Christian Contribution to New Labour',
   Sarpsborg, Norway, 28 September 2002.
5. Easter is a special time for Blair. In *New Britain: My Vision for
   a Young Country* (London: Fourth Estate, 1996) he wrote,
   'Easter, a time of rebirth and renewal, has a special
   significance for me and, in a sense, my politics. My vision of
   society reflects a faith in the human spirit and its capacity to
   renew itself' (quoted in Timms, 'Christian Contribution to
   New Labour').
6. Quoted in Timms, 'Christian Contribution to New Labour'.
7. Tom Baldwin, 'Please God, save us all from religion in
   politics', *Times*, 18 November 2004.
8. Joan Bakewell, 'The Christian lobby is flexing its muscles',
   Independent, 8 December 2006.

9. Quoted in Shane Brighton, 'British Muslims, Multiculturalism and UK Foreign Policy: "Integration" and "Cohesion" in and beyond the State', *International Affairs* (2007), vol. 83, pp. 1–17.

10. W. D. Rubinstein, *Capitalism, Culture, and Decline in Britain 1750–1990* (London: Routledge, 1993).

Chapter 6

1. Lewis Baston, presentation to Britain 2025 seminar, Defra, 2006.

2. See Anthony Downs, *An Economic Theory of Democracy* (New York: Harper, 1957).

3. Geoff Mulgan (ed.), *Life after Politics: New Thinking for the Twenty-First Century* (London: Demos, 1997).

4. Anthony Nutting, *No End of a Lesson: The Story of Suez* (London: Constable, 1967).

5. Matthew d'Ancona, 'A brief history of Blair', *Sunday Telegraph*, 19 November 2006.

6. Ibid.

7. John Van Wingen and Herbert K. Tillema, 'British Military Intervention after World War II: Militance in a Second-Rank Power', *Journal of Peace Research* (1980), vol. 27, pp. 291–303.

8. Michael Walzer, *Just and Unjust Wars: A Moral Argument with Historical Illustrations* (New York: Basic, 2000).

9. Tony Blair, speech to the Los Angeles World Council, 1 August 2006.

10. *Darfur: Indiscriminate Bombing Warrants UN Sanctions* (New York: Human Rights Watch, 2006).

11. C. A. R. Crosland, *The Future of Socialism* (London: Jonathan Cape, 1956).

12. A. J. P. Taylor, *English History 1914–1945* (Oxford: Clarendon Press, 1965).

Index

Cold War 40–1
Colley, Linda ix
consensus politics
  (1943–59) 54, 56–7, 80–1, 82, 86, 91
  (1959–79) 54–5
  (1979–92) 55, 57, 84–5
  (1992–2003) 55–6, 82–3, 91
  (2003–7) 56, 86–9, 91
  and Conservative Party 91–2
  critique of 54–5, 89–94
  definition of 53
  and Labour Party 91–2
Cook, Robin 150
Cooper, Robert 100
Crosland, Anthony 29, 66, 72–3, 159
cultural elitism 121–2
culturalism
  and decline debate 7–12, 13, 128
Culture of Contentment, The (Galbraith) 88

Daily Mail 6
Dalton, Hugh 82
Dance to the Music of Time, A (Powell) 36
d'Ancona, Matthew 140–1
Darfur, conflict in 151, 155–6, 157, 158
Davies, Norman x
Day that Britain Died, The (Marr) ix
decline debate
  and the Cambridge school 16–17
  and culturalism 7–12, 13, 128
  and defence of sterling 32–4, 54

and economics 7, 10, 24, 26–7, 32–4
and education 10
amongst electorate 5–6
end of, under Blair and Brown 4–5, 6–7, 13–14, 127–30
European comparisons 21–2, 78
and free-market right 25–9, 87–8, 128
German comparisons 20–1, 44
amongst historians 5, 15–18
and Keith Joseph 25–8
and left wing 29–32, 128
in literature 35–8
and Margaret Thatcher 4, 9, 13, 25, 28–9, 129
and public services 9, 29, 31–2
role of the elite 7–8, 18
role of the state 24, 27, 87
United States comparisons 21–2, 43
in the Victorian period 3
democracy, debate on 18–20
devolution 103–5
disarmament debate 98

economics
  and decline debate 7, 10, 24, 26–7, 32–4
  efficiency of Britain 42–4, 77–9
Edgerton, David 43–4
education
  and decline debate 10
electorate
  ageing 5–6, 132, 134–6
  apathy of 116–19, 131–7
  and Gordon Brown 65
  and social class 132–4
  trust in politicians 139–43